Writing Models

Writing Models Year 4
Pie Corbett
ISBN 1-84312-095-X

Writing Models Year 5
Pie Corbett
ISBN 1-84312-096-8

Writing Models Year 6
Pie Corbett
ISBN 1-84312-097-6

Jumpstart!
Key Stage 2/3 Literacy Games
Pie Corbett
ISBN 1-84312-102-6

Word Power
Activities for Years 3 and 4
Terry Saunders
ISBN 1-84312-141-7

Word Power
Activities for Years 5 and 6
Terry Saunders
ISBN 1-84312-142-5

Writing Models

Year 3

Pie Corbett

 David Fulton Publishers

This edition reprinted in 2010 by Routledge
2 Park Square, Milton Park, Abingdon, Oxon, OX14 4RN
Simultaneously published in the USA and Canada
By Routledge
270 Madison Avenue, New York, NY 10016

First published in 2004 in Great Britain by David Fulton Publishers

David Fulton Publishers is an imprint of the Taylor & Francis Group, an informa business

British Library Cataloguing in Publication Data
A catalogue record for this book is available from the British Library.

ISBN 1-84312-094-1

Designed and typeset by Kenneth Burnley, Wirral, Cheshire

Contents

Introduction

What does the book contain?

This is part of a series of books for use at Key Stage 2 that contain banks of photocopiable models for writing, covering the full writing range of poetry, fiction and non-fiction for pupils in Years 3–6.

For each text type a complete example has been provided. For some text types, there is also a supplementary extract focusing on a specific aspect of the text type, e.g. openings. Annotated copies of simpler examples provide key teaching points at a glance. There are also simple teachers' notes that give a swift outline of reading and writing activities linked to the examples. To help with differentiation we have included simpler and harder examples.

How to use the model texts to teach writing

Writing begins with reading. The more familiar children are with a text type, the more likely it is that they will be able to write in a similar vein. This is because children who read avidly will have internalised the patterns of language. When they come to write, they can then easily slip into the right 'voice' so that what they write 'sounds right'. It is not surprising that the best writers in a class are always children who read. So, any work on writing will always begin with reading plenty of examples.

You also need to provide plenty of opportunities to 'talk the text type', using the same sort of language. For instance, when working on narrative, story-telling helps many children to begin using the appropriate patterns of narrative language. If you are teaching them how to write recounts, then telling anecdotes will get the children into the 'right' voice.

Written text types	Oral text types
Narrative	Story-telling
Poetry	Poetry performance
Recount	Anecdotes
Explanation	Explaining
Report	Informing
Discussion	Debates
Persuasion	Arguing a viewpoint

Ideally, it helps if you can set up something interesting and motivating as a starting point for writing. This may involve first-hand experience, drama, video, music, art, a visit, and so on. Children will be more committed to writing if there is a purpose and some sort of genuine audience. Therefore it helps to publish writing through display, the school website, booklets, photocopied anthologies, etc.

Introduction

How to use this book

The models in this book can be turned into OHTs, or photocopied, to use in a variety of ways:

1 Analysis

Either as a whole class, in pairs or as individuals, encourage the children to read the text as writers and analyse the structure and language features.

To prepare for writing, look at the specific models provided in this book, analysing how they are structured and what language features are used. The annotated versions and teachers' notes will draw your attention to these. Try to avoid the temptation to tell the children but let them annotate the examples and work out as much as they can for themselves. A problem-solving approach is more likely to embed the learning! This analysis can be turned into a 'writer's toolkit' – a reminder sheet or wall chart that can be used during writing and referred to afterwards for self-evaluation and marking.

Before launching into writing, you may feel that the class needs to practise the spelling of certain key words. For instance, when working on traditional tales, learning how to spell 'once' would be handy! Furthermore, certain specific sentence structures might be needed for the text type you are working on, and these too could be rehearsed. For instance, you could try practising putting together opening lines, or writing sentences beginning 'Suddenly . . .', and so forth. These can be practised on mini-whiteboards. To find ideas for sentence and spelling games, see my book *Jumpstart!*, available from David Fulton.

2 Demonstration

You can use the models in this book to demonstrate how to write each of the text types. In the NLS video *Grammar for Writing* you can see teachers holding models in their hands or glancing at a model pinned up beside the board. While writing they talk through their decisions, rehearsing sentences, making alterations and rereading to check for sense and accuracy. When demonstrating, try to ensure that you make specific reference back to the models and the writer's toolkit. Demonstration is useful for any aspect of writing that is new, or that children find difficult. In demonstration, you are able directly to explain and show pupils how to write a text type.

3 Shared writing

Demonstration is usually followed by shared composition. Here, you act as scribe for the class or group, leaving them free to focus on the composition. This does not mean accepting any old contribution, but pushing the class to think for themselves and to evaluate their ideas. Weak vocabulary and sentence structure should be challenged. The class may need reminding to return to the model or check the writer's toolkit. In shared composition the teacher scaffolds the pupils' attempts. If children struggle with their own

Introduction

writing, then you will need to keep returning to shared writing, gradually handing over more and more of the decisions to the class.

4 Independent writing

Shared writing is usually followed by independent writing. Some children will still find it helpful to have a model to hand for reference as they write. Certainly the model, and the writer's toolkit, can be used for self-evaluation and marking. Some children may need extra support during shared writing – this might be through working with an adult, a partner, using a writing frame, a bank of vocabulary or sentence starters. However, the aim is for the majority to be able to write independently.

Guided writing can be used to teach at the point of writing – to support and challenge. If you find you are stretched for time, it may be more important to use guided time to focus on those who struggle. This means that class teaching can be aimed high.

5 Evaluation

After writing, children can self-evaluate. This might be carried out in pairs by using response partners. The author should read through his or her own writing, identifying strengths. He or she can then make selected improvements to the composition – as well as checking on accuracy.

If you are marking the work, try to keep your comments focused, indicating what has worked well and where improvements need to be made:

- Use a highlighter to highlight the best parts.
- Indicate where improvements are needed using symbols such as dotted lines, etc.

When work is returned, pupils should read what the teacher has written, sign it and then be given an opportunity to respond. There should be a range of improvements that each child can make, for example using a more powerful word, improving sentence structure, adding in more information, dropping in a clause, correcting punctuation, improving common spellings, etc. Your marking will also lead the following sessions as it should identify what has to be taught next.

Using technology

It can be helpful if several children write straight onto blank OHTs. This means that in the plenary, or the next day, these can be used for whole-class teaching – identifying strengths, checking against the models and toolkits and showing how to improve. If you have an interactive whiteboard then a child can compose straight onto the screen. I find it useful if the author will come out, read their own work through and explain what they are pleased with and discuss areas that might need further work. This evidently calls for some sensitive handling, though in the main most children enjoy their chance at the OHP!

Introduction

Why use a model?

Sometimes the reading material we use provides an ideal model. For instance, Kit Wright's poem 'Magic Box' works without fail to produce good quality writing. However, most adult writing for children is actually too subtle and complex to offer a model that can easily be imitated. To put it bluntly, Ted Hughes' *The Iron Man* is a great book to use with Year 3 children. But Hughes was a genius at level 3,000, and Darren aged 7³/₄ years is only at level 2! The specific models in this book provide clear structures that will support children's own writing. Those who struggle as writers should stick to imitating the models – while your most able pupils will have already internalised the patterns and should not be hindered from moving beyond.

Poetry models

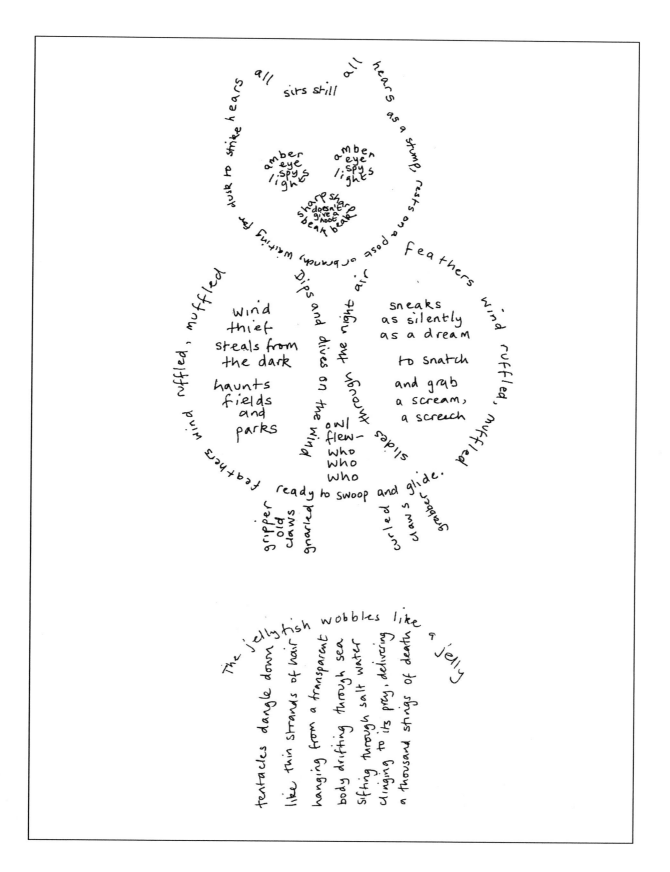

Candlelight

The match scratches,
Grazing the box,
Letting loose
the golden genie.

The flame slips
Onto the candle,
Fidgets restlessly,
Till it stills –

Like an amber eye,
A shy spy,
Stealing secrets
From the dark.

The flame flicks,
Winks once
And is gone –

Leaving a twist
Of sullen smoke
Above that still
White pillar.

Pie Corbett

Candlelight

The match scratches,
Grazing the box,
Letting loose
the golden genie.

The flame slips
Onto the candle,
Fidgets restlessly,
Till it stills –

Like an amber eye,
A shy spy,
Stealing secrets
From the dark.

The flame flicks,
Winks once
And is gone –

Leaving a twist
Of sullen smoke
Above that still
White pillar.

Pie Corbett

Poetry models

Candlelight

Begin poem with lighting the match

The **match** scra**tch**es,
Grazing the box,
Letting **l**oose
the **g**olden **g**enie.

Internal rhyme – sounds like a match scratching?

Alliteration – makes it sound memorable

Then light the candle

The flame **slips**
Onto the candle,
Fidgets restlessly,
Till it **stills** –

Makes the flame sound alive by getting it to do something – dance, skip, flicker, etc.

Rhyme

What does it look like? To generate similes draw flame shapes and ask what they look like, e.g.

Like an amber **eye**,
A **shy spy**,
Stealing secrets
From the dark.

Simile, followed by three rhymes

Alliteration

The **flame flicks**,
Winks once
And is gone –

Alliteration

Makes it sound like an eye

Now snuff the candle out

What is left?

Leaving a twist
Of **sullen smoke**
Above that **still**
White **pillar**.

Why is it sullen?

Rhyme

Pie Corbett

Candleflame

The candle flame
dances like a pony in a field.

The candle flame
twists like a hurricane spinning.

The candle flame
dodges like a thief hiding in the dark.

The candle flame
darts like an arrow to its end.

The candle flame
quivers like a trembling lip.

The candle flame
shivers like a cold, old man's hand.

Pie Corbett

I Remember . . .

Looking at the late-night taxis crawl like black beetles down Kings Street,
Looking at the street lights' broken reflection on the rainy pavements,
Looking at the boarded-up shop windows, the empty bus shelters, the
    queue from the chip shop winding out into the road, houses sitting in
    neat rows.

Tasting the salt of bacon straight from the grill,
Tasting the crunch of sugar that sits in a thick layer on a lardy cake,
Tasting the tang of lemon squeezed onto pancakes,
Tasting too much vinegar, drowning the chips!

Smelling the sweet taste of an illicit apple,
Smelling the cut grass on a hot summer's day,
Smelling the petrol, making rainbow patterns in a puddle,
Smelling the blocked drains in number forty-two . . .

Touching the knotted fur on my dog Sandy,
Touching the sudden cold of my Gran's frail hand,
Touching the icy railings on a winter morning . . .

Listening to the television mumbling below my room at night,
Listening to the sharp screech of brakes as a car halts,
Listening to my brother's breathing in the dark as he sleeps,
Listening to my own memories rattling in my mind.

Pie Corbett

My World

I like to look at
The cars cruising down the Western High Street,
The belisha beacon's yellow light at the crossing,
The distant tower blocks climbing high to the sky.

I like to listen to
The foghorn hooting down by the harbour,
The airplane zipping through the blue summery sky,
The steady thud of the disco beat.

I like the smell of
Hot tarmac when the sun is blazing,
Candyfloss twisting on a stick,
School dinners when I haven't had breakfast!

I like the taste of
A sweet mango that has been kept cool in the fridge,
Hot sundae sauce on ice cream,
Sherbet lemons fizzing in my mouth.

I like to touch
The warm fur of my purring cat,
Cold stones on a hot day,
A hot-water bottle when the frost settles.

Pie Corbett

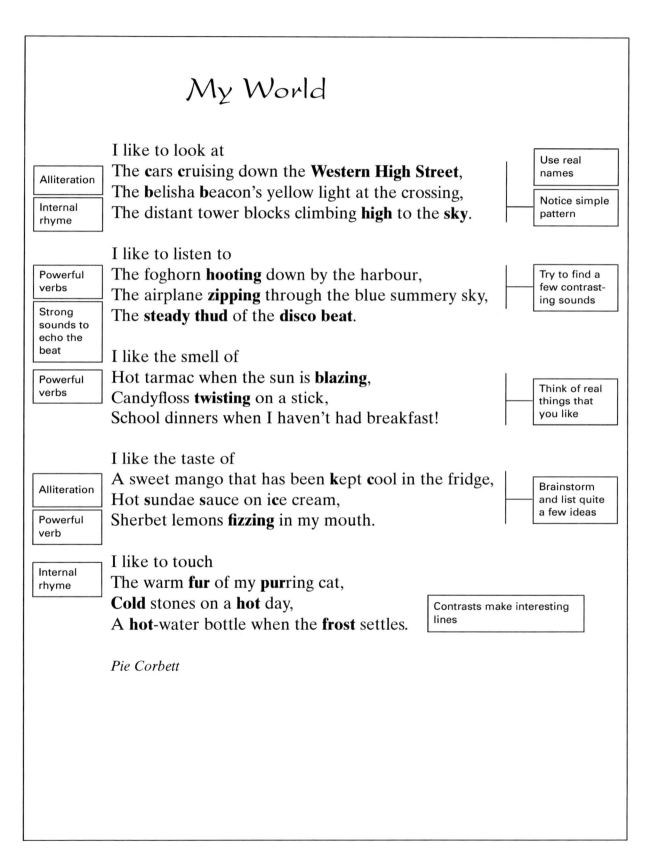

My World

Alliteration

Internal rhyme

I like to look at
The **c**ars **c**ruising down the **Western High Street**,
The **b**elisha **b**eacon's yellow light at the crossing,
The distant tower blocks climbing **high** to the **sky**.

Use real names

Notice simple pattern

Powerful verbs

Strong sounds to echo the beat

Powerful verbs

I like to listen to
The foghorn **hooting** down by the harbour,
The airplane **zipping** through the blue summery sky,
The **steady thud** of the **disco beat**.

I like the smell of
Hot tarmac when the sun is **blazing**,
Candyfloss **twisting** on a stick,
School dinners when I haven't had breakfast!

Try to find a few contrasting sounds

Think of real things that you like

Alliteration

Powerful verb

I like the taste of
A sweet mango that has been **k**ept **c**ool in the fridge,
Hot **s**undae **s**auce on i**c**e cream,
Sherbet lemons **fizzing** in my mouth.

Brainstorm and list quite a few ideas

Internal rhyme

I like to touch
The warm **fur** of my **pur**ring cat,
Cold stones on a **hot** day,
A **hot**-water bottle when the **frost** settles.

Contrasts make interesting lines

Pie Corbett

7

The Travelling Salesman's Scottish Song

Spent a while
in Argyll.

Was quite cute
in Bute.

Won some cash
in Cat's Ash.

Felt free
in Dundee.

Froze
in Montrose.

Chased a thief
in Crieff.

Thought of Paris
while on Harris.

Felt a fool
on Cairn Toul.

Caught a cough
at Cape Wrath.

Felt like hell
in Yell

and decided
to go home . . .

Pie Corbett

A Chance in France

'Stay at home',
Mum said,

But I,
took a chance
in France,
turned grey
for the day
in St Tropez,
forgot
what I did
in Madrid,
had some tussels
in Brussels
with a trio
from Rio,
lost my way
in Bombay,
nothing wrong
in Hong Kong,
felt calmer
in Palma,
and quite nice
in Nice,
yes, felt finer
in China,
took a room
in Khartoum
and a villa
in Manila,

had a 'do'
in Peru
with a llama
from Lima,
took a walk
in New York
with a man
from Milan,
lost a sneaker
in Costa Rica,
got lumbago
in Tobago,
felt a menace
in Venice,
was a bore
in Singapore,
lost an ear
in Korea,
some weight
in Kuwait,
tried my best
as a guest
in old Bucharest,
got the fleas
in Belize
and came home.

Pie Corbett

The Zealous Zoo

The loud lion lazily laughed at the lost leopard.

The horrid hippo happily hobbled to the hairy heron.

The tired tiny tigers tearfully told a terrifying tale of torture.

The mischievous monkey meanly made massive mistake.

The cool, calm cobra quietly collected a cluttered cauldron of coins.

The lively, lonely locust lovingly lapped the lemon juice.

The poorly paid panda politely picked a prickly pear with its pink paw.

Pie Corbett

Collective Poem

Have you heard?
Have you heard?
Of the common word –

A sloth of bears,
A leash of hares,

A mischief of rats,
A clutter of cats,

A knot of frogs,
A drift of hogs,

A bunch of grapes,
A shrewdness of apes,

A swarm of eels,
A crash of seals.

But what about –

A scold of jays,
A week of days,
A kindle of kittens,
A comfort of mittens,
A charm of finches,
A ruler of inches,
A shiver of sharks,
A shimmer of sparks,
A knot of toads,
A map of roads,
A herd of yaks,
A scream of smacks?!

Pie Corbett

The Obstinate Ostrich

The silent swift
slips through
the sheer blue.

A bald blackbird
boldly stabs
the hard soil,
toiling to tug
that tasty worm.

The serene eagle
slowly settles
on the harsh
rocky ledge.

The jenny wren
sits in the hedge,
sips from the dew,
and flutters
her dreary wings.

The obstinate ostrich
hides its head
below the sand
and waits till danger
passes by . . .

Pie Corbett

Poetry models

The Obstinate Ostrich

The silent **swift**
slips through
the sheer blue.

Note alliteration in each verse

A **bald** blackbird
boldly stabs
the **hard** soil,
toiling to tug
that **tasty** worm.

Try to select interesting adjectives

The serene eagle
slowly settles
on the harsh
rocky ledge.

The occasional adverb may help

The jenny wren
sits in the hedge,
sips from the dew,
and **flutters**
her dreary wings.

Use powerful verbs

The obstinate ostrich
hides its head
below the sand
and waits till danger
passes by . . .

Think about how each bird behaves

Pie Corbett

Nonsense Poem

I went to the stiggler fair.
The broggarts and braggs were there.
By the light of the shoon,
the bold spadoon
was scrunging his golden glare.

The shabbler fell out of his spotter,
slid down the torgid's cotter;
the spanger sleezed
and fell on his knees.

But what became of the chunky,
chunky, chunky, chunk?!

Pie Corbett

Animal Riddle

My first is in tea but not in meal.
My second is in pinch but never in feel.

My third is in grab but not in hold.
My fourth is in blame but never in scold.

My last is in brush but not in a comb.
There's a clue in the zoo but never at home.

Pie Corbett

Story models

'What's up?' snarled Tim.
'Not much,' replied Bill.

'Pass the sugar,' Mrs Jenkins said quietly.
'No way,' Simon snapped rudely.

'I smell wet dog,' snapped Mr Warbox, grabbing his umbrella.
'Leaping lizards,' muttered Annie, trying to hide Benji.

'Get out,' snarled Jazz. She grabbed the door and flung it wide open. But Brand stood his ground. Outside they could hear the crowd shouting.
'Keep your hair on,' retorted Brand.

'The donuts are ready to eat,' said Mrs Ramsbotham. She grinned at her family as she placed the dish on the table with a flourish. Mr Ramsbotham glanced up from his newspaper and winced. The grandfather clock chimed twelve.
'Oh no, not more donuts,' he sighed.

Story models

'What's up?' **snarled** Tim.
'Not much,' **replied** Bill.

> Use a well-chosen speech verb that suggests how the speaker is feeling

'Pass the sugar,' Mrs Jenkins said **quietly**.
'No way,' Simon snapped **rudely**.

> A well-chosen adverb can add extra information about how something is spoken

> Add in a supporting action by using an 'ing' clause

'I smell wet dog,' snapped Mr Warbox, **grabbing his umbrella**.
'Leaping lizards,' muttered Annie, **trying to hide Benji**.

> What the speaker did

'Get out,' snarled Jazz. **She grabbed the door and flung it wide open.** *But Brand stood his ground.* **Outside they could hear the crowd shouting.**
'Keep your hair on,' retorted Brand.

> The listener's reaction

> Background detail

> What the speaker did

'The donuts are ready to eat,' said Mrs Ramsbotham. **She grinned at her family as she placed the dish on the table with a flourish.** *Mr Ramsbotham glanced up from his newspaper and winced.* **The grandfather clock chimed twelve.**
'Oh no, not more donuts,' he sighed.

> The listener's reaction

> Background detail

The Giant Man

She turned and looked across the fields towards the hill. Beyond the fence was the rolling gold of the corn. Beyond the corn ran a distant hedge of gorse that bloomed like bright sulphur. Beyond the hedge towered the high hill. On the hill grew a circle of trees. Standing in the trees was the giant. His hair was hardly visible as his head was tangled in the branches where the rooks cawed and the squirrels darted.

Strawberry Banks

Strawberry Banks is a field near the school. To get there you have to cross a stile and walk through a small piece of woodland. Then you come out onto the top of the bank. The field is on a hillside and it stretches down into the valley. There are no roads and no houses so it seems like a secret place, tucked away from human eyes.

In the summer you can smell the wild thyme and hear the bees buzz. There are patches of yellow gorse that smell like coconut. On the way down, there are mole hills and lots of tiny tracks. These paths are where the sheep walk. If you sit still you are bound to see rabbits, and high in the sky you will see a kestrel hovering.

Story models

The Giant Man

Useful opening

Introduce surprising character in setting

She turned and looked across the fields towards the hill. **Beyond** the fence was the rolling gold of the corn. **Beyond** the corn ran a distant hedge of gorse that bloomed like bright sulphur **Beyond** the hedge towered the high hill. On the hill grew a circle of trees. **Standing in the trees was the giant**. His hair was hardly visible as his head was **tangled** in the branches **where** the rooks **cawed** and the squirrels **darted**.

Use repetition to build description

Powerful verbs

Use 'where' to add in more detail

Strawberry Banks

Name familiar place

What is it?

Strawberry Banks is a **field** near the school. **To get there** you have to cross a stile and walk through a small piece of woodland. Then you come out onto the top of the bank. The field is on a hillside and it stretches down into the valley. There are no roads and no houses so it seems like a secret place, tucked away from human eyes.

How do you get there?

Use your senses

In the summer you can **smell** the wild thyme and hear the bees buzz. **There** are patches of yellow gorse that smell like coconut. On the way down, there are mole hills and lots of tiny tracks. These paths are where the sheep walk. If you sit still you are bound to see rabbits, and high in the sky you will see a kestrel hovering.

What can you see?

Story models

In a distant valley lived a giant.

Mitch Buggins was a most unusual boy.

Once upon a time there lived a baker who told lies.

Billy Bolt jumped over the fence and into Mr Gargery's garden where he was not allowed.

'Do you think it's safe to touch?' asked Tiny, glancing nervously at the terrier.

One cold, crisp wintry morning Jan decided that it was time to use her magic powers.

Story models

| Prepositional phrase | **In a distant valley** lived a giant. |

| Name of character | **Mitch Buggins** was a most unusual boy. |

| Traditional and character flaw | **Once upon a time** there lived a baker **who told lies**. |

| Put character into a forbidden place | Billy Bolt jumped over the fence and into Mr Gargery's garden **where he was not allowed**. |

| Question opening | **'Do you think it's safe to touch?'** asked Tiny, glancing nervously at the terrier. |

| Set the scene | **One cold, crisp wintry morning** Jan decided that it was time to use her magic powers. |

And so they all lived happily ever after.

The giant made his way back to that distant valley and was never heard of again.

Billy knew that he should never have gone into Mr Gargery's garden. But if he hadn't, then the diamond would never have been found!

As for Mitch, he promised his mother that he would never fly again. But I'm afraid to say that when he made the promise, he had his fingers crossed!

At that moment the sun came out. The sea was quite calm now and people began to wander back onto the beach. Jan smiled to herself, knowing that all was well once again.

Tiny whistled and the terrier came bounding over, its tail wagging crazily. So it was that Tiny found a new friend and forgot his fear of dogs!

Story models

Traditional	And so they all lived happily ever after.
Take main character back to where they started	The giant made his way back to that distant valley and was never heard of again.
Explain what the character has learned	Billy knew that he should never have gone into Mr Gargery's garden. **But** if he hadn't, then the diamond would never have been found!

Use 'But' to add an extra edge

End with main character talking to an adult about what they have learned	As for Mitch, he promised his mother that he would never fly again. **But** I'm afraid to say that when he made the promise, he had his fingers crossed!
Use the weather to indicate all is well. Show how character feels	At that moment the sun came out. The sea was quite calm now and people began to wander back onto the beach. Jan smiled to herself, knowing that all was well once again.
Provide contrast at end so character is happy, finds a new friend and is better for the experience!	Tiny whistled and the terrier came bounding over, its tail wagging crazily. So it was that Tiny found a new friend and forgot his fear of dogs!

Story models

One Sweet Too Far

Alfie Crackmell was the smallest boy in his class. All his school career he had been called all sorts of names – Titch, Tiny, Midget. Today he didn't care about that because he had something in his pocket that he was not allowed. It was a large bag of sweets. His uncle Derek had given them to him that morning. His Mother did not allow him to have sweets because she said that they would rot his teeth. Alfie didn't care. His teeth looked fine to him and besides, who could resist a packet of fruity gumdrops?

Alfie ran out into the playground and made his way up to the top end by the old bike sheds. No one hung around up there because it smelt and was cold. Alfie didn't care. He just wanted to be alone so that he could taste a gumdrop. The packet was rather sticky and as he opened it he could smell the sweets. He tugged out a large, red gumdrop and popped it into his mouth. He had meant to see how long he could make it last but within a moment he was chewing madly, his teeth sticking together.

Suddenly, he heard a noise behind him. He turned round, and leaning on the side of the old sheds was Billy Boon. The two boys eyed each other. They had never been friends.

'Gimme one,' muttered Billy, taking a step forwards. Alfie knew that it was no good running. Billy was not only the largest boy in the school but also the fastest. He hadn't got a chance. Alfie dug his hand into his pocket and pulled out what was there. It was an old piece of chewing gum that he had found stuck under his table in the classroom. He had been saving it up for emergencies.

'Here,' said Alfie, holding the gum out. Billy grabbed it and shoved it into his mouth. As soon as his tongue felt the cold, hard lump he knew that Alfie had cheated him, but as he was about to grab him, a voice blurted out, 'Are you chewing, Billy?'

There was silence as Mr Barsby made Billy open his mouth wide, checked to see the contents and then made him spit the gum into a bin. Alfie stood by and watched with glee. After all, chewing in school was forbidden. Sweets were not healthy, and Billy should have known better.

24

Story models

One Sweet Too Far

Main character has something special	Alfie Crackmell was **the smallest boy** in his class. All his school career he had been called all sorts of names – Titch, Tiny, Midget. Today he didn't care about that because **he had something in his pocket** that he was not allowed. It was a large bag of sweets. His uncle Derek had given them to him that morning. His Mother did not allow him to have sweets because she said that they would rot his teeth. Alfie didn't care. His teeth looked fine to him and besides, who could resist a packet of fruity gumdrops?	Opening
Main character is enjoying himself	Alfie ran out into the playground and made his way up to the top end by the old bike sheds. No one hung around up there because it smelt and was cold. Alfie didn't care. He just wanted to be alone so that he could taste a gumdrop. The packet was rather sticky and as he opened it he could smell the sweets. He tugged out a large, red gumdrop and popped it into his mouth. He had meant to see how long he could make it last but within a moment he was chewing madly, his teeth sticking together.	Build-up
Connective used to introduce dilemma	**Suddenly** he heard a noise behind him. He turned round and leaning on the side of the old sheds was Billy Boon. The two boys eyed each other. They had never been friends.	
	'Gimme one,' muttered Billy, taking a step forwards. Alfie knew that it was no good running. Billy was not only **the largest boy** in the school but also the fastest. He hadn't got a chance. Alfie dug his hand into his pocket and pulled out what was there. It was an old piece of chewing gum that he had found stuck under his table in the classroom. He had been saving it up for emergencies.	Problem
Alfie tries to trick Billy		
An adult intervenes	'Here,' said Alfie, holding the gum out. Billy grabbed it and shoved it into his mouth. As soon as his tongue felt the cold, hard lump he knew that Alfie had cheated him, but as he was about to grab him, **a voice blurted out, 'Are you chewing, Billy?'**	Resolution
Tongue-in-cheek moral	There was silence as Mr Barsby made Billy open his mouth wide, checked to see the contents and then made him spit the gum into a bin. Alfie stood by and watched with glee. **After all, chewing in school was forbidden. Sweets were not healthy, and Billy should have known better.**	End

25

You Can Have Your Cake . . .

It was a cold wintry day. Mitch Biggins stuffed his PE clothes into his school bag and glared at Mr Barsby. He hated games and in the winter it was sheer torture! Mr Barsby waved his hand to dismiss the class and they trooped out onto the darkening streets. Mitch had things to do after school. His Mum had told him that very morning not to loiter. He had to go straight round to the corner shop, pick up a cake and come home.

'Your auntie Doreen is coming for tea and she loves coffee cake.'

It was getting dark now and the corner shop was lit up. It was warm inside. Mrs Jenkins smiled at Mitch as she tucked the cake into a white box and slipped it inside a blue carrier bag.

'Now, you go carefully,' she said.

Mitch nodded and headed off for home. He didn't really like his auntie that much. She always ruffled his hair and called him 'young man'. But he knew that he had to be home on time or his Mum would be upset. By now she would have laid out the best tea things. They would be having sticky buns, crumpets and fish-paste sandwiches. Mitch hated fish paste but he loved hot crumpets, dripping with butter and honey. The coffee cake would take pride of place in the centre of the table. He paused and sniffed the bag. The smell of sweet coffee was so strong that you could almost taste it.

As Mitch came to the corner of Hearn Street, he saw them. It was Slugger Clarke and his mob. They were waiting for him by the broken fence that led onto the strip of wasteland.

'Here Mitch,' called out Slugger. The next thing Mitch knew, he was surrounded. Someone shoved him over and soon they had him pinned down.

'Get off you lot,' shouted Mitch, but it was no good. Two of them were sitting on his back. He squirmed round till he could just see Slugger picking up the carrier bag and sniffing the contents.

'Mmm, this smells mighty good, and there's just enough for all of us.'

'Get off,' spluttered Mitch, 'that's for my Auntie Doreen.'

'Well, I'm sorry matey, but it looks like your Auntie is going to have to go hungry,' replied Slugger. Then there was a pause while the others laughed mockingly.

'That is, unless you care to walk the plank for our amusement?' He had no choice really. Either he walked the plank or he had to go home with no cake. He could just see it – his mother's disappointment and disbelief and Auntie Doreen tutting around him.

Two minutes later they were all on the wasteland, standing by the plank. It hung out over a stagnant pool where the mosquitoes danced in the summer. Now that it was winter, there was a thin skin of ice covering the slime.

'You promise you'll give it back,' said Mitch as he began to walk.

There was a laugh from behind him but he ignored it. He had to concentrate. Step by step, he walked further out along the plank. As he moved along, his weight began to make it bend and he knew that one false move and he would topple in.

The surface looked dark and uninviting. It was thick with green scum and oily patches. In fact it wasn't too hard to reach the end but turning was difficult. Mitch paused and carefully edged round. Then he began to walk back, his heart pounding. He was going to make it! But Slugger had other plans for him. Seeing that Mitch was not going to fall in, he decided to shake him off. So Slugger climbed onto the plank and began making it wobble by shifting his weight from side to side.

Mitch kept quite still and held his arms out so that he could keep balance. Slugger came further down the plank, taunting Mitch and calling him names.

'You've got no dad,' sneered Slugger and that was one step too far. Mitch had noticed a small log sticking up out of the water. It looked as if it had lodged firm. He jumped from the plank onto the log and skipped onto the bank in one swift movement. As he did this, with the sudden release of his weight, the plank pinged up and sent Slugger flying into the water. He landed with a satisfying smack, face down, flat in the green scum.

Mitch grabbed the bag and dashed through the fencing back onto Hearn Street. At first he thought that they would give chase, but they were too busy dragging their leader out of the pond.

As Mitch pounded down the street, clutching the bag as tightly as he could, he thought that he could hear the sound of crying. He couldn't resist a little grin. Mr Barsby had been right about one thing. The hop, skip and jump had been worth learning after all.

Story models

Scene 1

The right-hand side of the stage is the hallway to a Victorian town house. Halfway across the stage is an imaginary door. The left-hand side of the stage is the pavement of a busy street. A small, scruffy boy is knocking at the door.

Bobby   Anybody there?

Mrs Savage   Now then, now then, who on earth is making all that fuss?

Bobby   Open up.

Mrs Savage   *(As she opens the door)* What do you want?

Bobby   I've come about the boilers, Miss.

Mrs Savage   Ah, so you're Gargery's boy. Well, you'd better come in.

Bobby   *(Coming into hall)* Thanks, Miss.

Mrs Savage   Hands!

Bobby   Djou what?

Mrs Savage   Hold out your hands. Turn them over. As I thought. They're filthy. Don't touch anything or I'll have you scrubbing. Now wait here and I'll send the housemaid down. She'll show you where to go.

Bobby   Yes, Miss.

Mrs Savage exits. Bobby gazes round him till Mabel, the housemaid, enters.

Mabel   Oooo, you are grubby.

Scene 1

The right-hand side of the stage is the hallway to a Victorian town house. Halfway across the stage is an imaginary door. The left-hand side of the stage is the pavement of a busy street. A small, scruffy boy is knocking at the door.

| | Scene-setting; instructions |

Bobby   Anybody there?

Mrs Savage Now then, now then, who on earth is making all that fuss?

Bobby   Open up.

| Stage instructions |

Mrs Savage *(As she opens the door)* What do you want?

Bobby   I've come about the boilers, Miss.

Mrs Savage Ah, so you're Gargery's boy. Well, you'd better come in.

Bobby   *(Coming into hall)* Thanks, Miss.

Mrs Savage Hands!

Bobby   **Djou** what?

| Use spelling to suggest accent |

Mrs Savage Hold out your hands. Turn them over. As I thought. They're filthy. **Don't touch anything** or I'll have you scrubbing. Now wait here and I'll send the housemaid down. She'll show you where to go.

| Makes audience think he will touch something |

Bobby   Yes, Miss.

Mrs Savage exits. Bobby gazes round him till Mabel, the housemaid, enters.

Mabel   Oooo, you are grubby.

| Emphasises how dirty he is |

31

While they are talking a postman comes up to the door and starts to search through his bag.

Bobby   I just come to do the boilers, that's all. Mr Gargery says they've got to be cleaned cos they've blocked up with the soot. He knows, Mr Gargery does, he's the best sweep there is in town, he is.

The postman knocks

Mabel   Stand just here and don't you do nothing. *(She opens the door and curtsies)* Good morning.

Postman   Here you are young lady, there's an important parcel for the master. It's come all the way from India by the look of it. Special Delivery, it is.

Mabel   Thank you, I'm sure.

Postman   Now you make sure that goes straight to your master.

Mabel   Yes, sir.

(The postman leaves)

Mabel   Look at that. I said 'Look,' not touch. You keep your hands to yourself.

Bobby   Didn't mean nothin' by it. Was just looking.

Mabel   P'raps it's a diamond necklace for the mistress.

Bobby   Yea, and p'raps it's an elephant's toenail. Come on, I ain't got all day to hang about while you daydream. Show us the boilers and I can get on.

Mrs Savage *(from off stage)* Mabel, come here at once!

Mabel   Now just you waits here. *(She puts the package down and leaves).*

Story models

While they are talking a postman comes up to the door and starts to search through his bag.

		Double action – both sides of the door

Bobby   I just come to do the boilers, that's all. Mr Gargery says they've got to be cleaned cos they've blocked up with the soot. He knows, Mr Gargery does, he's the best sweep there is in town, he is.

The postman knocks

Mabel   Stand just here and don't you do nothing. *(She opens the door and curtsies)* Good morning.

Postman   Here you are young lady, there's an important parcel for the master. It's come all the way from India by the look of it. Special Delivery, it is.

Emphasises how important parcel is

Mabel   Thank you, I'm sure.

Postman   Now you make sure that goes straight to your master.

Mabel   Yes, sir.

(The postman leaves)

Mabel   Look at that. **I said 'Look', not touch.** You keep your hands to yourself.

Hints that he might touch

Bobby   Didn't mean nothin' by it. Was just looking.

Mabel   P'raps it's a **diamond necklace** for the mistress.

Makes audience think that perhaps it is precious

Bobby   Yea, and p'raps it's an elephant's toenail. Come on, I ain't got all day to hang about while you daydream. Show us the boilers and I can get on.

Mrs Savage *(from off stage)* Mabel, come here at once!

Mabel   Now just you waits here. *(She puts the package down and leaves).*

Audience left wondering if he will touch parcel and what it might contain

The Magic Brush

Long, long ago in China there lived a poor boy called Chang. He loved drawing. He was too poor to have a paint brush so he used a stick. He would draw in the sand or scratch marks on walls.

One day when Chang was by the river, he saw a large, silver fish trapped in the reeds by the riverbank. The fish was struggling to get free. Chang felt sorry for the fish so he helped to release it.

Later that day Chang was sleeping. In his dream a man dressed in a silver cloak spoke to him. 'You are a kind boy Chang. I am giving you a magic brush. Use it to help the poor.' Chang woke with a start, and lying beside him was a paint brush.

So Chang painted the shape of a butterfly in the earth. It changed into a real butterfly and flew away. Chang was amazed with his gift and ran straight back to the village to see how he could help the poor people.

He painted a donkey for the young mother to help her carry her goods. He painted an ox to help the farmer pull his plough. He painted a hoe for the old lady to weed her garden. Every day he found a new use for the paint brush.

The emperor heard of Chang and his magic brush. He sent for Chang and ordered him to paint a field of golden corn. Chang didn't want to obey the greedy emperor so he drew a sea with a tiny island in the distance.

'Where is my field of gold?' shouted the emperor.

'Just here,' replied Chang, drawing a tiny field on the island.

'Paint me a boat so that I can travel to the island,' snarled the emperor. So Chang painted a boat. The emperor climbed onto the boat. Chang drew the north wind blowing towards the island.

'I'm going too slowly,' roared the emperor. 'Paint stronger wind.'

So Chang drew a storm. The waves grew rougher until the boat capsized and the emperor disappeared. And Chang drew a white horse so that he could ride home and tell his friends what had happened to the emperor who wanted too much for himself.

Story models

The Magic Brush

Long, long ago in China there lived a poor boy called Chang. He loved drawing. He was too poor to have a paint brush so he used a stick. He would draw in the sand or scratch marks on walls.

> Opening – introduces character

One day when Chang was by the river, he saw a large, silver fish trapped in the reeds by the riverbank. The fish was struggling to get free. Chang felt sorry for the fish so he helped to release it.

> Act of kindness

Later that day Chang was sleeping. In his dream a man dressed in a silver cloak spoke to him. 'You are a kind boy Chang. I am giving you a magic brush. Use it to help the poor.' Chang woke with a start, and lying beside him was a paint brush.

> Kind act is repaid with a gift

So Chang painted the shape of a butterfly in the earth. It changed into a real butterfly and flew away. Chang was amazed with his gift and ran straight back to the village to see how he could help the poor people.

He painted a donkey for the young mother to help her carry her goods. He painted an ox to help the farmer pull his plough. He painted a hoe for the old lady to weed her garden. Every day he found a new use for the paint brush.

> How main character uses the gift

The emperor heard of Chang and his magic brush. He sent for Chang and ordered him to paint a **field of golden corn.** Chang didn't want to obey the greedy emperor so he drew a sea with a tiny island in the distance.

> Powerful figure wants a greedy wish

'Where is my field of gold?' shouted the emperor.

'Just here,' replied Chang, drawing a tiny field on the island.

'Paint me a boat so that I can travel to the island,' snarled the emperor. So Chang **painted a boat.** The emperor climbed onto the boat. Chang drew the north wind blowing towards the island.

> Main character cheats powerful figure

'I'm going too slowly,' roared the emperor. 'Paint stronger wind.'

So Chang drew a storm. The waves grew rougher until the boat capsized and the emperor disappeared. And Chang drew a **white horse** so that he could ride home and tell his friends what had happened to the emperor who wanted too much for himself.

> End

Side notes:

- Useful strong connectives
- What other greedy character might this be?
- What else might be wished for?
- What else could be drawn to get rid of nasty character – a fog, a river, a trap?
- What could you escape on?

The King of the Fishes

Once upon a time there lived a poor fisherman called Li.

Every day he went down to the shore. There he stood on the rocks and threw the nets into the icy waters and waited. When he pulled the nets in, he would take any fish back to the market and sell them.

One day he caught a huge fish. It had silver scales that glittered red and gold. It was so beautiful that Li stood amazed, staring at the fish as it thrashed about in the net. Li suddenly felt guilty. It was so beautiful, and surely it must have a family . . .

So he scooped the fish up and set it free. Li stood watching as the fish swam out to sea. Then to his amazement, it turned and spoke to him.

'Li, you have saved the King of the Fishes. I grant you one wish. Come back here when the moon is high in the sky and tell me what you would like.' With that, the King of the Fishes was gone.

Immediately, Li hurried home, wondering what on earth he should wish for. There were so many things that his family needed.

First he asked his old father. 'Father, if you had one wish, what would it be?' There was a silence and then his father said, 'Why son, I would wish for new eyes, for I am blind and will never see again.'

Next he asked his old mother. 'Mother, if you had one wish, what would it be?' There was a silence and then his mother said, 'Why son, I would wish for money, for the roof needs mending and the winter winds whip through the house and make my bones shiver so.'

Finally he asked his wife. 'Wife, if you had one wish, what would it be?' There was a silence and then his wife said, 'Why Li, I would wish for a baby, for who will care for us when we are old? Yes, nothing would be more precious than a child.'

Poor Li could not make up his mind – they needed the money certainly, but then his father was blind and that was a terrible thing. He also knew that a child would bring such joy to them all.

All evening Li paced up and down trying to decide what the wish should be.

Suddenly, he stopped pacing and grinned. Yes, he had it! He rushed out of the house, through the forest and down to the sea. The moon was high in the sky and so it was the time to talk to the King of the Fishes. Li ran down onto the rocks and stood there with the foam crashing about him. He could see the moon's reflection on the waves, and then there was the King of the Fishes.

'What do you wish for, Li?' called the king in his high, silvery voice.

'I wish for my father to see our son in a cradle made of gold,' shouted Li. There was a silence and the great fish disappeared. The waves stilled and Li could see the stars like silvery freckles in the dark night sky. Then out of the darkness he heard a noise, drifting down through the forest. It was a baby crying . . .

The Fox and the Raven

Once upon a time Raven found a piece of cheese. Whose cheese it was we do not know, and besides it does not matter. Raven stole that slice of cheese and flew off, thinking about his slice of luck. He had been hungry and now he had a huge chunk of cheese to devour. I suppose that somewhere in the forest there was a hunter who was about to find that his cheese had been stolen.

So Raven flew up to his favourite tree. He sat on his favourite branch and began to eat the cheese.

Suddenly Fox came by. Now Fox was hungry because he had not eaten for two days. He looked up at Raven and saw the cheese. He licked his lips. How he wanted that cheese. But Raven had it firmly in his beak and was not going to let go.

'Raven, Raven, you have such beautiful black flight feathers,' said Fox. Raven was pleased that Fox admired him so much.

'Raven, Raven, you have such beautiful shiny tail feathers,' said Fox. Raven was pleased that Fox admired him so much.

'Raven, Raven, you have such a beautiful curved beak,' said Fox. Raven was pleased that Fox admired him so much.

'Raven, Raven, you have such beautiful sharp talons,' said Fox. Raven was pleased that Fox admired him so much.

'Raven, Raven, surely someone as beautiful as you must have a beautiful voice,' said Fox. Raven shook his head and opened his beak to sing for Fox and to show him just how very beautiful his voice was. Of course the cheese fell out of his beak and as it tumbled to the ground Fox opened his jaws and the cheese fell straight into his mouth.

Raven let out a croak. Fox chewed on the cheese and ran off. For they do say that a flatterer is no real friend.

The Fox and the Raven

Once upon a time Raven found a piece of cheese. Whose cheese it was we do not know and besides it does not matter. Raven stole that slice of cheese and flew off, thinking about his slice of luck. He had been hungry and now he had a huge chunk of cheese to devour. I suppose that somewhere in the forest there was a hunter who was about to find that his cheese had been stolen.

So Raven flew up to his favourite tree. He sat on his favourite branch and began to eat the cheese.

Suddenly Fox came by. Now Fox was hungry because he had not eaten for two days. He looked up at Raven and saw the cheese. He licked his lips. How he wanted that cheese. But Raven had it firmly in his beak and was not going to let go.

'Raven, Raven, you have such beautiful black flight feathers,' said Fox. Raven was pleased that Fox admired him so much.

'Raven, Raven, you have such beautiful shiny tail feathers,' said Fox. Raven was pleased that Fox admired him so much.

'Raven, Raven, you have such a beautiful curved beak,' said Fox. Raven was pleased that Fox admired him so much.

'Raven, Raven, you have such beautiful sharp talons,' said Fox. Raven was pleased that Fox admired him so much.

'Raven, Raven, surely someone as beautiful as you must have a beautiful voice,' said Fox. Raven shook his head and opened his beak to sing for Fox and to show him just how very beautiful his voice was. Of course the cheese fell out of his beak and as it tumbled to the ground Fox opened his jaws and the cheese fell straight into his mouth.

Raven let out a croak. Fox chewed on the cheese and ran off. For they do say that **a flatterer is no real friend**.

Story connectives

A creature finds a tasty morsel and begins to eat

A hungry, cunning creature comes by

The hungry creature uses flattery.
Notice the repetitive pattern

The trick!

Simple moral

The Mouse and the Lion

Some say that mice fell to earth from the clouds during a storm. Others say that white mice bring good luck. The great Roman philosopher Pliny recommended mouse ashes mixed with honey as a mouth wash. But the story I have to tell you is about this tiny creature and one of the most powerful creatures – the lion.

One night, Mouse was out hunting. He wasn't thinking about what he was doing and he wasn't looking where he was going when he blundered into Lion. Lion had been fast asleep but in a moment he whacked his great paw down and trapped Mouse in one blow.

Mouse looked so small and Lion wasn't really hungry.

'Please don't eat me. Think of my children,' pleaded Mouse. Lion thought of his own children and decided to let him go. Mouse rushed off into the forest, his heart beating madly.

Later that night Lion was trapped by hunters. They threw a net over him so that he was fixed to the ground and could not move. Mouse was still out hunting when he came to the place where Lion was trapped.

Poor old Lion, thought Mouse. He began to nibble at the ropes that held Lion pinned down. One by one the ropes snapped free till in the end Lion was able to wriggle out from under the net.

While the hunters slept, Lion and Mouse ran off into the forest, both free and friends. For they do say that the strong may be weak and the weak may be strong, but kindness is a strength that all may own.

Why Spider Has a Small Waist

It was harvest time. Spider loved this time of year. All the villages held parties and Spider was always invited. That year he received invitations to two parties on the same day.

This was a problem. Spider loved eating and there was no way that he was going to miss out. So he found two pieces of rope and tied one end of each round his waist. Then he asked Monkey to take a loose end to each of the two villages.

'Tell the strongest men there to give a tug on the rope once the feast begins,' said Spider, licking his lips. 'As soon as I feel a pull on the rope, I'll run over and join in the feast. Then I'll dash back to the other village. That way I won't miss out!'

Well, the harvest days arrived. The villagers set out their feasts, and soon everyone was dancing and singing in celebration. It just so happened that they both settled down to eat at the same time.

Spider was waiting in the forest halfway between both villages. Imagine his surprise when he felt a tug on both ropes at the same time. The men tugged and tugged, for it seemed as if the rope was stuck and Spider did not appear. Poor Spider was being pulled in both directions, and who knows how long he stood there with the ropes squeezing his middle so that his waist grew thinner and thinner as the ropes tightened.

That is why the spider has a thin waist. It is also why the spider waits for its food to come into its web. Spider doesn't like to go visiting any more!

How the World Was Made

Once upon a time there was no sun, no moon, no stars. There was only darkness.

On the first day of the week the piper began to bang his great bass drum and the mountains appeared, one by one.

On the second day of the week the piper began to play his flute and the rivers flowed down the hills and into the sea.

On the third day of the week the piper began to bang his silver cymbals and the forests appeared, flowing like water over the land.

On the fourth day of the week the piper began to play his violin and the grasses grew and swept like waves across the earth.

On the fifth day of the week the piper began to strum his guitar and with each note a new creature appeared.

On the sixth day of the week the piper began to click his castanets and man and woman appeared in the forest.

On the last day of the week the piper began to sing and as the piper sang the sun, the moon and finally the stars appeared one by one in the great open skies.

So the world began.

How the World Was Made

Once upon a time there was no sun, no moon, no stars. There was only darkness.

| Simple repetitive pattern |

On the first day of the week the piper began to bang his great **bass drum** and the mountains appeared, one by one.

| Change instrument each day |

On the second day of the week the **piper** began to play his flute and the rivers flowed down the hills and into the sea.

On the third day of the week the piper began to bang his silver cymbals and **the forests appeared**, flowing like **water over the land**.

| Each instrument creates something new |

On the fourth day of the week the piper began to play his violin and **the grasses grew** and swept like **waves across the earth**.

On the fifth day of the week the piper began to strum his guitar and with each note a new creature appeared.

On the sixth day of the week the piper began to click his castanets and man and woman appeared in the forest.

On the last day of the week the piper began to sing and as the piper sang the sun, the moon and finally the stars appeared one by one in the great open skies.

| Save the most dramatic for last |

| Punchy ending | **So the world** began.

Dear Tiger

You will never guess what has happened.

Spider has been greedy once too often. You know how he always manages to rush around at harvest time, dashing from one village to another making sure that he gets well fed wherever he goes. This year his greed got the better of him and now he has the slimmest waist of them all!

Why, his waist is slimmer than Snake's! He looks so funny with his eight spindly legs sticking out from his brown body. His waist is tucked in and his body bulges out.

It is a lesson for us all — don't get too greedy!

Best wishes

Monkey

Story models

Dear Tiger

You will never guess what has happened.

It is useful to list character words, e.g. 'jealous', 'mean', 'happy'

Spider has been **greedy** once too often. You know how he always manages to rush around at harvest time, dashing from one village to another making sure that he gets well fed wherever he goes. This year his greed got the better of him and now he has the slimmest waist of them all!

How he behaves

Why, his waist is slimmer than Snake's! He looks so funny with his eight spindly legs sticking out from his brown body. His waist is tucked in and his body bulges out.

What he looks like

It is a lesson for us all — don't get too greedy!

Best wishes

Monkey

Dear Cousin

Do you remember the fisherman Li? He was the young man who lived in the forest down near the sea. Let me remind you by explaining what he looks like. He is a handsome lad with dark hair. He has very blue eyes. Li is strong and he needs to be because he has to pull in his nets and cast them out into the sea.

He is one of the hardest workers that I ever met. He gets up early every day and goes down onto the beach. He spreads the nets out to let them dry in the sun. Then he casts them out from the rocks. When he has caught enough fish he wraps them up in palm leaves and packs them into baskets to take to market.

His house is a ramshackle old wooden building in the forest. He lives there with his wife and parents. They are very poor and the house is almost falling down! His poor father is blind and cannot help Li with the fishing.

Well, the most amazing thing has happened because Li and his family have come into money. Yes, they are rich! This all happened because Li was kind enough to spare the life of the King of the Fishes and he was well rewarded with one wish! He was clever enough to wrap three wishes into one so now his father can see, his wife has a baby and they have enough money to last more than a lifetime.

So, dear cousin — kindness pays!

Lots of love from

Your loving cousin

The King of the Fishes

Once Li had money he was able to mend the roof. His father started to help him on the beach mending nets. His wife looked after the baby. All was well.

Every day Li went down to the beach with his father. They set out the nets to dry. His father sat on the rocks and mended the nets while Li caught the fish. His father would help to pack the fish into baskets to take to the market.

One day Li trapped a dolphin. It lay in the net squeaking and Li set it free. He watched as it swam out towards its family. They bobbed up and down in the waves waving their flippers. Li knew that he had made another friend.

That afternoon Li set out in his little wooden boat. He was going to look at his lobster pots in the next bay.

Suddenly, a sea serpent appeared. It coiled itself around the little wooden boat and began to squeeze. The wooden timbers creaked and with an enormous crack the little boat shattered into pieces. Li was left swimming for his life with the serpent behind him. It opened its mighty jaws and its tongue flickered towards Li.

At that moment the dolphins appeared, weaving through the water as if they were sewing it together. They sped towards Li and one of them bobbed up underneath him. Li wrapped his arms round the dolphin's neck as they sped for safety.

Eventually they reached the shore and Li's father was amazed to see his son riding on the back of a dolphin. Li waved to his father and his father waved back. His son was safe and there were fish in the baskets to take to the market. Yes, all was well.

The Magic Brush

Once Chang had found the magic brush you can be certain that he was very popular. He was able to help all the villagers.

One day he was out in the fields helping everyone to bring in the harvest. The sun was blazing and they were lying by the hedge, eating bread and cheese.

Suddenly, they heard a terrible noise. It was a giant wandering across the country. He was enormous, with a head the size of a barrel and eyes like cartwheels. They all watched as the giant trampled on the harvest. He paused and began to put all the goats into an enormous sack.

So Chang took out his magic brush. In the mud he scratched a picture of a Chinese dragon. He painted the wind dragon. No sooner had he painted the wind dragon than it appeared. It swooped down at the giant and blew him right over. The giant began to crawl away as fast as he could. The dragon flapped its wings so that the giant's hair streamed in the gale. The dragon breathed fire and singed the giant's clothes.

Finally, the giant disappeared. Everyone crept out from under the hedge. They were all delighted that the giant had gone, but the fields were ruined. So Chang drew a landscape of fields ready for the harvest. Everyone got back to work and Chang tucked his magic brush away.

Story models

The Magic Brush

Simple five-part story: • opening; • build-up; • problem; • resolution; • ending. Note use of story connectives to introduce each point

Once Chang had found the magic brush you can be certain that he was very popular. He was able to help all the villagers.

One day he was out in the fields helping everyone to bring in the harvest. The sun was blazing and they were lying by the hedge, eating bread and cheese.

> All is well

Suddenly they heard a terrible noise. It was a giant wandering across the country. He was enormous, with a head the size of a barrel and eyes like cartwheels. They all watched as the giant trampled on the harvest. He paused and began to put all the goats into an enormous sack.

> Introduce a monster!

So Chang took out his magic brush. In the mud he scratched a picture of a Chinese dragon. He painted the wind dragon. No sooner had he painted the wind dragon than it appeared. It swooped down at the giant and blew him right over. The giant began to crawl away as fast as he could. The dragon flapped its wings so that the giant's hair streamed in the gale. The dragon breathed fire and singed the giant's clothes.

> Magic is used to defeat monster

Finally, the giant disappeared. Everyone crept out from under the hedge. They were all delighted that the giant had gone, but the fields were ruined. So Chang drew a landscape of fields ready for the harvest. Everyone got back to work and Chang tucked his magic brush away.

Examples of Openings

Time

Once upon a time there was a forgetful giant called Frank who had to wear glasses.

Early one rainy morning a rat crept into Connor Macarthy's house and fell asleep in his shoe. It was only looking for shelter but it got more than it bargained for!

It was a dark wintry night when Jennifer Jackson won the ice skating competition.

On Sunday morning at half-past nine Mrs Boom discovered Billy's collection of earwigs that he had hidden in the fridge.

Settings

At the end of the lane stood an old house where no one was allowed to play.

They say that in Hangman's Wood there are ghosts. Petie Fisher didn't believe that tale. That is, not until he went walking there.

The pond was quite still except for the odd ripple where the midges danced.

The cliff was higher than Josh had expected. He turned and looked back at the advancing sea and knew that climbing was the only way to escape.

Character

Mrs Savage strode into the classroom and eyed Class 3 menacingly.

Danny was wearing a long, black cloak, shiny red shoes and a wizard's hat.

Gary Metcalf was not a nice boy.

Story models

Examples of Openings

Time

Note use of time openings

Once upon a time there was a **forgetful** giant called Frank **who had to wear glasses**.

Unusual detail to intrigue reader

Early one rainy morning **a rat** crept into **Connor Macarthy's house** and fell asleep in his show. It was only looking for shelter but it got more than it bargained for!

Introduce a creature into an unlikely place

It was a dark wintry night when Jennifer Jackson **won the ice skating competition**.

But will she be happy?

On Sunday morning at half-past nine Mrs Boom discovered Billy's collection of earwigs that he had hidden in the fridge.

Adult discovers a secret!

Settings

Prepositional phrase

At the end of the lane stood an old house where no one was allowed to play.

Name suggests it's a frightening place

They say that in ***Hangman's Wood*** there are ghosts. Petie Fisher didn't believe that tale. **That is, not until he went walking there.**

We now know what is going to happen

The pond was quite still except for the odd ripple where the midges danced.

Calm opening

The cliff was higher than Josh had expected. He turned and looked back at the advancing sea and knew that climbing was the only way to escape.

Dangerous setting

Character

Mrs **Savage strode** into the classroom and eyed Class 3 **menacingly**.

Three clues to suggest she is not in a good mood

Descriptive sentence of three things

Danny was wearing a **long, black cloak, shiny red shoes and a wizard's hat**.

Gary Metcalf **was not a nice boy.**

Open with a negative about your character

Further Examples of Openings

Action

'Just jump,' yelled the voice.

The two boys began to run as fast as they could.

The Rottweiler was only just behind them.

Tim screamed as the rope snapped.

Suspense

Jan woke with a start.

Jazzy peered down the dark alley. Something was coming towards her.

The night was quite dark and still. Then somebody screamed.

Mood

The sun sparkled on the waves as they lapped the shore. In the distance an ice-cream van jingled. The blue sky seemed to stretch on for ever. Julie leaned back in her deckchair and grinned.

The wind whipped down the street sending leaves and rubbish flying. Rain lashed down, drumming on rooftops and goose-pimpling the road. Water gurgled in the gutters. Lightning crackled, flaring in the darkness. At number 42 an open door was banging and no one seemed to notice.

Story models

Further Examples of Openings

Action

Being chased starts story with a bang	'Just jump,' yelled the voice.
	The two boys began to run as fast as they could.
The 'monster'	The **Rottweiler** was only just behind them.

Use short sentences to create dramatic openings

Tim **screamed as the rope snapped**.

Something drama-toc happens

Suspense

Short, dramatic sentence: makes reader wonder what woke her

Jan woke with a start. | Frightening setting |

Jazzy peered down the **dark alley**. **Something** was **coming** towards her.

Empty words to let imagination wonder

Bland opening

The night was quite dark and still. **Then somebody screamed.**

Then introduce dramatic noise or event

Mood

Note powerful verbs

The sun **sparkled** on the waves as they **lapped** the shore. In the distance an ice-cream van **jingled**. The blue sky seemed to **stretch** on for ever. Julie **leaned** back in her deckchair and **grinned**.

Gentle, calm setting

Note how description builds up around 'wind', 'leaves', 'rubbish', 'rain', 'water', 'lightning'

The wind whipped down the street sending leaves and rubbish flying. Rain lashed down, drumming on rooftops and goose-pimpling the road. Water gurgled in the gutters. Lightning crackled, flaring in the darkness. At number 42 an open door was banging and no one seemed to notice.

Active, dramatic setting

TERM 3: **FIRST-PERSON ACCOUNT OF INCIDENT IN STORY READ**

I ran out of the front door and heard the key click in the lock. From inside, I could hear my aunts squabbling as they began to count all the money.

I wandered down the garden to where the peach was growing. It was dark, and high in the sky was the moon looking like a great silvery peach.

The shadows seemed to become creatures of the night. I felt a shiver of fear so I walked down towards the peach. It seemed to be larger than ever, like a glistening, pink moon sitting in the garden. The grass was wet with dew and I left a trail of footprints. Suddenly, I could feel magic tingling in the air and I knew that something amazing was going to happen.

I clambered over the fence and walked right up to the peach. I pressed my cheek against its soft sides. It felt smooth and slightly furry. It was then that I noticed a small hole like a doorway in the side of the peach.

It was late one evening when it happened. I was fishing in the little stream over by Calder, where it runs down into the sea. It was getting dark and I had already snagged my line in the reeds several times so I decided to stop.

I wandered up through the woods. Further up the valley the owls were hooting and I paused to listen. Ahead of me was the ghostly sound of the owls, and behind me the slow rush of the sea.

It was then that it happened. At first I thought that it was just my imagination but I was sure that I was being watched. I could feel the hairs on the back of my head prickle. Then I turned to look up to the top field where it meets the cliff's edge. That was where I saw it. Two huge green lights as if someone had parked a bus up there.

As I was staring, I saw the lights move up. Against the darkening sky, I could see the outline of a massive giant with green, glowing eyes. It was taller than a building. It stood there for a moment with the wind singing through its fingers. I'd had enough by then as you can imagine. What with the owls hooting and then seeing this figure! I started to run and I didn't stop till I got home.

Simple Plan for a Mystery Story

Chapter 1 – the children see something mysterious.
Chapter 2 – they go to investigate.
Chapter 3 – they get trapped.
Chapter 4 – they try to escape.
Chapter 5 – they get caught.
Chapter 6 – they get away.

THE MYSTERY OF THE LANTERN LIGHT

Chapter 1

Amy Johnson hated having to walk the dog but every night it was the same story. Her mum would ask her to take Sam down to the bottom of the lane and back.

Outside it was dark, the moon covered by the clouds. Amy shivered as she walked down towards the bottom of the lane. She was just passing the old church hall when she noticed a light, flickering in the window. She stopped by the fence and tugged Sam away from a tree that he had been sniffing.

Amy knew that the church hall was never used on a Tuesday evening. She had walked past the hall every Tuesday for at least four years and there had never been anybody there before. She crouched down and pulled Sam close to her.

She could just see the light – it was a lantern, an old-fashioned lantern and someone was waving it back and forth as if they were signalling. Suddenly, the lantern went out and she heard the faint sound of a crash as if someone had broken some glass.

Amy waited a while and then tugged Sam by the collar back up the lane. After a few steps she let her fear get the better of her and she ran as fast as she could all the way home.

Story models

THE MYSTERY OF THE LANTERN LIGHT

Chapter 1

Amy Johnson hated having to walk the dog but every night it was the same story. Her mum would ask her to take Sam down to the bottom of the lane and back.

> Opening introduces main character

Outside it was dark, the moon covered by the clouds. **Amy shivered** as she walked down towards the bottom of the lane. She was just passing the old church hall when she noticed a light, flickering in the window. She stopped by the fence and tugged Sam away from a tree that he had been sniffing.

> Shows how she feels

> Take main character somewhere lonely – where she sees/hears something out of place or mysterious

Amy knew that the church hall was never used on a Tuesday evening. She had walked past the hall every Tuesday for at least four years and there had never been anybody there before. She crouched down and pulled Sam close to her.

She could just see the light – it was a lantern, an old-fashioned lantern and someone was waving it back and forth **as if they were signalling**. Suddenly, the lantern went out and she heard the faint sound of a crash as if someone had broken some glass.

> Suggests danger

> The mystery deepens with a sound!

Amy waited a while and then tugged Sam by the collar back up the lane. After a few steps she let her fear get the better of her and she ran as fast as she could all the way home.

> Main character runs – and the mystery remains to be solved

The Mystery of the Ottoman's Chest

Chapter 1

Class 3 had just finished visiting the Egyptian room in the museum. Brian sat down on the bench in the corridor and began to eat his sandwiches. He watched the others troop off to find the museum shop. His Mum hadn't sent him with any money so there was no point in going along with them.

He chomped his way through a peanut butter sandwich and then tucked into an apple. He'd saved the Mars bar till last. While he was chewing on the Mars bar he noticed two men nip into a room further down the corridor. At first Brian thought nothing of it, but a moment later one of them looked out of the door as if he was checking that no one was coming.

Brian felt uneasy so he stood up and hid behind a tall suit of armour. He could still see down the corridor to the room where the two men were. What on earth were they up to? He finished the Mars bar and just as he was beginning to think that he was being silly, the man glanced out again, looking up and down the corridor. Brian froze.

A moment later the men came out of the room and went off down the corridor in the opposite direction, moving as fast as they could. Between them they were carrying a large, old trunk and it had to be quite heavy because they were struggling. Every so often they had to pause, put the trunk down and rest. At the end of the corridor, Brian saw them push the trunk into a lift and then the doors closed and the trunk and men disappeared.

At that moment an alarm bell began to ring madly and a museum attendant staggered out of the room from where the men had appeared. He was clutching his head as if he had been hit. Brian kept as still as he could. He certainly did not want to get involved in anything unpleasant. It was bad enough having a Mum who gave no pocket money and peanut butter sandwiches as a packed lunch, without getting involved in anything nasty. He stood still and waited for the bell to stop.

The BFG

The *BFG* is an incredible book written by the world-famous author Roald Dahl. Though it was written many years ago the story is still just as inventive and fresh as it must have seemed when it was first published.

The story is about an orphan called Sophie who befriends a friendly giant. The pair of them try to get the Queen of England on their side because terrible giants are coming to eat the children.

I liked the way that at the start of the story Sophie is lonely but by the end she has found a friend. I also found the way the giant speaks very amusing. Roald Dahl uses lots of invented words such as 'gizzardgulper' and 'whizzpopping' (which is extremely rude)! It is almost as if he invents a new language for the giant to speak. This makes the book both amusing and thought-provoking.

In conclusion, this is an amazing adventure written for primary school children which makes excellent reading.

The Iron Man

The Iron Man is an amazing book written by Ted Hughes.

The story is about a boy called Hogarth who discovers an iron man. The Iron Man is destroying the land and Hogarth finds a clever way to tame the Iron Man and give him something useful to do. In the second half of the book the world is about to be attacked by a space creature and the Iron Man comes to the rescue.

I liked the first half of the book best of all because it was so frightening and realistic. The second half of the book seemed like a separate story and was not so interesting as Hogarth was not really involved. Also, I think it was an unlikely ending with the space dragon singing.

In conclusion, this is a well-written book that all Year 3 children would enjoy reading.

The Iron Man

The Iron Man is an amazing book written by Ted Hughes.

Introduce the book and the author

The story is about a boy called Hogarth who discovers an iron man. The Iron Man is destroying the land and Hogarth finds a clever way to tame the Iron Man and give him something useful to do. In the second half of the book the world is about to be attacked by a space creature and the Iron Man comes to the rescue.

A brief recount of what happens – not too much detail

I liked the first half of the book best of all because it was so frightening and realistic. The second half of the book seemed like a separate story and was not so interesting as Hogarth was not really involved. Also, I think it was an unlikely ending with the space dragon singing.

Likes and dislikes

In conclusion, this is a well-written book that all Year 3 children would enjoy reading.

Conclusion and who would enjoy this

Non-fiction models

Unicorns

A unicorn is a type of horse with a horn.

Unicorns all look the same. They have the body of a horse and a long horn. The horn sticks out from the middle of its head. It has a sharp point and is usually a spiral shape. Most unicorns are a pure white. Some red and black unicorns have been seen.

Unicorns usually live in forests. They are very shy and like to hide in the trees so that they cannot be seen. In the daytime they keep well hidden but as the sun goes down and at dawn they move around.

Did you know?
In 1673 a man called Dr Olfert Dapper said that he had seen a unicorn while walking in the woods.

They eat grass like ordinary horses and drink water. If you want to see a unicorn you could stay by a pool where you have seen a unicorn's hoof-prints! Some unicorns also eat apples and carrots.

Unicorns are best known for the magic contained in their horns. Evil people kill unicorns and cut off the horns. These are then used as magic wands. If you meet a unicorn, it will probably tell you that it is the last one left on earth. Hopefully, this will not be true!

True or False?
If a unicorn's horn is dipped into poison-ous water it will become pure. (True)

The most amazing thing about unicorns is that they are very rare and if you meet one it could bring you great luck.

Non-fiction models

Unicorns

A unicorn is a type of horse with a horn.

| What it is (definition) |

Unicorns all **look** the same. They have the body of a horse and a long horn. The horn sticks out from the middle of its head. It has a sharp point and is usually a spiral shape. Most unicorns are a pure white. Some red and black unicorns have been seen.

| What it looks like |

Use present tense to make it sound as if they exist!

Unicorns usually **live** in forests. They are very shy and like to hide in the trees so that they cannot be seen. In the day-time they keep well hidden but as the sun goes down and at dawn they move around.

| Where it lives |

They eat grass like ordinary horses and drink water. If you want to see a unicorn you could stay by a pool where you have seen a unicorn's hoof-prints! Some unicorns also eat apples and carrots.

| What it does |

Unicorns are best known for the magic contained in their horns. Evil people kill unicorns and cut off the horns. They are then used as magic wands. If you meet a unicorn, it will probably tell you that it is the last one left on earth. Hopefully, this will not be true!

| More interesting information |

Talk to the reader

The most amazing thing about unicorns is that they are very rare and if **you** meet one it could bring you great luck.

| Best fact saved for end |

Did you know?
In 1673 a man called Dr Olfert Dapper said that he had seen a unicorn while walking in the woods.

| Use 'True' or 'False' boxes to add in 'Did you know . . .' facts |

True or False?
If a unicorn's horn is dipped into poisonous water it will become pure. (True)

Dragons

A dragon is a fire-breathing monster.

There are many different kinds of dragons. They vary in size from those that are only as small as a bat, to the largest which are bigger than an elephant. Nearly all have wings and can fly great distances. Their skin tends to be leathery and so tough that it is hard for an arrow or spear to even make a mark. Many have shiny scales that are tougher than steel. They look rather like massive crocodiles with long tails. They have huge jaws and jagged teeth for eating meat. Dragons are usually red, green or black, though there have been dragons spotted that are different colours. They breathe fire and smoke!

Dragons are found across the world. The majority like to live well away from humans. In the main they live in caves, high up on hills or mountain ranges. They sleep for long periods of time, preferably in the cool darkness of their inside lodgings.

Unfortunately dragons have been known to eat human beings. In the main they prefer to eat cattle or sheep. They will also swoop down and catch deer and other small creatures. They only eat humans as a final resort. Dragons are best known for hoarding treasure. This they keep inside their caves, piled into a huge mound. They usually sleep on top of the treasure so that no one can steal it. It is not a good idea to try to steal from a dragon! They live to a great age and are considered to be very wise. However, they do not have human feelings and can seem quite cruel. They fear knights but love princesses!

Five amazing facts about dragons.
- **Some have the head of a lion or eagle.**
- **In India there is an elephant-dragon.**
- **Some dragons live in lakes.**
- **They live in fear of St George.**
- **Chinese dragons are friendly (but like presents!).**

The most amazing thing about dragons is that they can be tamed and become a household pet (well – you need a castle really)!

How to Make a Traditional Story

Making a traditional story is easy enough if you have the right ingredients. You should follow the steps listed below and if you do, you too can invent stories to keep your friends amazed and amused.

What you need: a farmer's daughter, a forest, a prince, a castle, an axe, night time, a wolf.

What you do:

1. First place the farmer's daughter alone in the forest.
2. Next boil the story gently as the prince looks out of the castle window and sees the girl.
3. After that add in the prince picking up an axe and going to find her.
4. Then stir in night and a hungry wolf.
5. Leave the story to cook for a while.
6. Now introduce a pinch of excitement by letting the wolf seize the girl!
7. Finally finish the story off by sprinkling in the prince, the axe and a sad end for the wolf!

As you can see, it doesn't take much to make a traditional tale. Of course, if the tale is to last then it will need that final, special ingredient – your imagination!

> *Extra tips:*
> **Add in a layer of complication by letting the prince lose his way!**

> *Further suggested ingredients:*
> **A lonely giant, a spiteful guard, a deep lake and something scary living in a cave in the middle of the forest.**

How to Trap a Troll

If you have a troll living in your area then you will need these instructions. No one wants a nasty troll nearby. So, read on and soon you will be able to scare off any troll that might be making your life a misery.

What you need: a large sack, plenty of tasty food, a clearing in a forest near the troll's cave, sunshine!

What you do:

1. First of all go into the forest and find the troll's cave.

2. Next find a clearing near the cave where it is sunny.

3. After that take the sack and fill it with tasty food.

4. Then just one minute before sunrise leave the sack in the clearing.

5. Now wake the troll by shouting 'Food!' loudly.

6. Finally, hide nearby and watch!

If you are lucky the troll will wake up and run outside. Trolls are very greedy so it will smell the food and run over to the sack. If you are lucky it will start eating. A few seconds later the sun will come up and the troll will be turned to stone!

Extra tips!

• **Keep well hidden as trolls are fierce.**

• **Be careful in case there are two trolls, and you don't see the second one till it's too late.**

Non-fiction models

How to Trap a Troll

If you have a troll living in your area then you will need these instructions. No one wants a nasty troll nearby. So, read on and soon you will be able to scare off any troll that might be making your life a misery.

> Opening introduces reader to subject matter

What you need: a large sack, plenty of tasty food, a clearing in a forest near the troll's cave, sunshine!

> What you need

> Note colon and commas in list

What you do:

> What to do

1. **First** of all *go* into the forest and find the troll's cave.

2. **Next** *find* a clearing near the cave where it is sunny.

3. **After** that *take* the sack and fill it with tasty food.

4. **Then** just one minute before sunrise *leave* the sack in the clearing.

5. **Now** *wake* the troll by shouting 'Food!' loudly.

6. **Finally**, *hide* nearby and watch!

> Use of numbers and time connectives

> Keep sentences clear and simple to help the reader

> Note instructional tone

If you are lucky the troll will wake up and run outside. Trolls are very greedy so it will smell the food and run over to the sack. If you are lucky it will start eating. A few seconds later the sun will come up and the troll will be turned to stone!

> Ending – wraps instructions up!

Extra tips!

- Keep well hidden as trolls are fierce.
- Be careful in case there are two trolls, and you don't see the second one till it's too late.

> Use 'extra tip' boxes and diagrams to help reader understand

Letter About Hare and Tortoise's Race

'The Burrow',
Western Warren,
Rabbitown,
Fableshire.

Dear Jack Rabbit,

Yesterday Mrs Badger and I went out to watch the hare race against the tortoise.

In the morning we all went down to the starting line and waited for the hare and the tortoise.

First of all Hare appeared. He was ready to run the race! He kept doing press-ups and sprinting up and down the path to practise his sprint start.

After a long while Tortoise appeared. He was walking very slowly. Some of the younger bunnies had to be told off for giggling. It certainly looked as if he had no chance at all.

When everyone was ready and the two animals were on the starting line, old owl said, 'Ready, steady, go!' and they both began the race.

Soon Hare could not be seen. Tortoise plodded on down the woodland path but everyone shook their heads. Mrs Badger had told him that he was silly to have made a bet with Hare. Everyone knows that Hare is the fastest animal in the great woods.

That afternoon we waited in the shade of the trees. Nothing happened for a long time. Just as we were thinking of giving up and going home we all saw Tortoise coming up the path. We were amazed. No one could believe it. Tortoise crossed the line and won the race.

Later on we heard that Hare had been so certain that he was going to win that he had lain down for a sleep!

It served Hare right for being so boastful about his speed!

Well, give my love to Mrs Rabbit and all your young ones.

From your old friend — Brock Badger.

Non-fiction models

Letter About Hare and Tortoise's Race

'The Burrow',
Western Warren,
Rabbitown,
Fableshire.

Dear Jack Rabbit,

Yesterday Mrs Badger and I went out **to watch the hare race against the tortoise.**

| Set the scene for the reader – when, who and what? |

In the morning we all went down to the starting line and waited for the hare and the tortoise.

| Use of time connectives to organise events in a sequence |

First of all Hare appeared. He was ready to run the race! He kept doing press-ups and sprinting up and down the path to practise his sprint start.

After a long while Tortoise appeared. He was walking very slowly. Some of the younger bunnies had to be told off for giggling. It certainly looked as if he had no chance at all.

| Add in detail to keep reader interested |

When everyone was ready and the two animals were on the starting line, old owl said, 'Ready, steady, go!' and they both began the race.

Soon Hare could not be seen. Tortoise plodded on down the woodland path but everyone shook their heads. Mrs Badger had told him that he was silly to have made a bet with Hare. Everyone knows that Hare is the fastest animal in the great woods.

| Use verbs to suggest character |

That afternoon we waited in the shade of the trees. Nothing happened for a long time. Just as we were thinking of giving up and going home we all saw Tortoise coming up the path. We were amazed. No one could believe it. Tortoise crossed the line and won the race.

| Give your views |

Later on we heard that Hare had been so certain that he was going to win that he had lain down for a sleep!

It served Hare right for being so boastful about his speed!

Well, give my love to Mrs Rabbit and all your young ones.

| Addresses reader |

From your old friend – Brock Badger.

| Friendly ending |

Tortoise's Diary – Monday

Today was the day of the race.

I got up early and rushed down to the starting point.

When I got there Owl started the race.

As soon as Owl said 'Go!', Hare rushed off down the path. I just kept going.

Later in the afternoon I was surprised to see Hare fast asleep at the side of the road. I crept past him and rushed on.

When I crossed the finishing line everyone cheered.

I was very happy to win. It serves Hare right for boasting.

Hare's Diary – Monday

Well, this has certainly been the WORST day of my life.

I set out early this morning and was at the starting line well before Tortoise. I mean, he is so slow! Of course, by the time he turned up, I had already done 300 press-ups and practised my speed sprint start.

Owl began the race and pretty soon I was halfway round. To tell the truth I wasn't even running very quickly. Anyway, I knew that I was going to win so I lay down at the side of the road for a snooze.

I still can't believe it. Tortoise carried on while I was asleep. It is SO unfair. He carried on running and came first.

When I finished the race there was Tortoise. HE HAD WON! Oh!, the shame!!

From 'The Encyclopaedia of Nasty Creatures'

Scorpions

Scorpions are not the same as insects but are a type of spider! They have eight legs like spiders. There are about 600 different types of scorpion. They live by catching insects. They have pincers rather like a crab. They use these to hold their prey. They kill their prey with the poisonous sting in the tip of their tail. They usually come out at night to feed, and hide during the day in the dark places. Their favourite meal is woodlouse. They live in warm places across the world.

Snakes

Snakes are reptiles. They have no legs. Their skin is covered in scales. There are over 3,000 different types of snake. There are no snakes in Ireland! They eat small animals. Some bite their prey and have poisonous fangs. Some snakes just open their mouths and swallow their prey! Snakes lay eggs. Many are harmless but snakes such as cobras are deadly.

Tarantula

Tarantulas are spiders. They are commonly known as the wolf spider. There are many different types of tarantula. Most grow to about 2.5 cms across and have hairy legs. Some have poisonous fangs which they use to kill their food. They live in the south-west of America, Mexico and South America. They do not spin a web but use their speed to seize their prey. Tarantulas hunt at night.

From the Long-lost 'Rough Guide to Fantasyland'

A

Alleys should be treated with caution by any traveller. Never go down an alley alone. They are usually dark and there will be someone hiding there ready to attack you.

Ambushes may happen at night or when you are not expecting to be attacked. It could be by bandits or goblins.

Amulets are made of precious metal and can be worn around the arm or neck to protect you.

B

Bandits will attack you in the hills. They will steal but not kill.

Beggars often turn out to be a wizard or prince in disguise.

Bets should never be taken, especially if they involve rolling dice or cards which will turn out to be enchanted. You are bound to lose!

Blacksmiths are handy for forging dwarf metal into powerful swords.

Boatsmen are not what they seem. Never take the oar from a boatsman as they are enchanted and you will have to row back and forth for a thousand years.

Boots may well have magical properties and can walk a thousand leagues.

C

Caves may make good hiding places. Travellers can seek shelter in mountain caves when on a journey. Beware of falling asleep in a cave in case goblins have a secret door at the back. Remember that dragons store treasure in caves!

Cloaks are often magical. Do not set off on your adventure without an invisibility cloak. Keep your face hidden by pulling the hood down.

Teachers' notes

POETRY MODELS

Notes for page 1: shape poems

Reading
- What are the different poems about?
- Look carefully at the words that have been chosen for each subject – note their relevance to the subject.

Writing
- With the class, decide on a subject, e.g. tree.
- Make a list of possible words that could be used to describe different parts of the tree – include some verbs, e.g. 'branches sway'.
- On a board draw a faint outline of a tree and then demonstrate how to insert words onto the outline to create the shape poem.
- Everyone completes their own 'tree' shape poem before designing their own. It may be handy to suggest possible subjects, e.g. rain, clouds, TV aerials, door, car, watch, book, TV set, computer, dog, cat, etc.

Notes for page 2: observation poems ('Candlelight')

Reading
- Read the poem through several times.
- Either work as a class to annotate or let the children annotate and then come together.
- Draw attention to key aspects – internal rhymes, alliteration, well-chosen words, simile.
- Discuss the effect of the poem – how does it make the candle seem?

Writing
- Light a candle and observe.
- Brainstorm words to describe the flame, the shadows, the wax, the wick, the candle, the lighting, the extinguishing.
- Demonstrate how to use these to create a thin candle poem, e.g. 'The thin flame/balances on the candle/dipping side to side/like a hot knife/slicing the darkness/like a dancer/dressed in golden silks . . .'

Notes for page 4: observation poems ('Candleflame')

Reading
- Draw attention to the use of interesting words (verbs) to show how the candle moves: can the children find all of these, and where do they come in the poem (start of each line)?
- Notice and discuss the different similes.
- Ask the children to explain the pattern.

Writing
- Light a candle and look carefully at how it moves.
- Brainstorm other verbs that might be used to describe how the flame moves, e.g. 'shimmers', 'gleams', 'glows', 'glitters', 'wobbles', 'wavers', etc.
- Work as a class and write several lines showing how to use the verb and add in a simile. Don't worry too much about the similes – just add one in, e.g. 'The candle flame/glows like a lamp in the dark'.

Notes for page 6: senses poems ('My World')

Reading
- Read the poem through – discuss where children agree/disagree.
- Annotate well-used words – 'cruising', 'zipping', 'blazing', 'fizzing', etc.

Writing
- List possible likes under each sense, giving time for the sharing of memories.

Teachers' notes

- Look carefully at the simple pattern that the different poems use.
- Demonstrate how to turn each idea into an interesting sentence, choosing words with care, e.g. 'I like to listen to the sound of the diggers tearing up the earth . . .' or 'Listening to the diggers tearing up the earth'.

Notes for pages 8 and 9: performance poems ('The Travelling Salesman's Scottish Song' and 'A Chance in France')

Reading
- Both poems read aloud well if chanted. This may take a bit of practice!
- Let children prepare readings in groups – maybe working as a class on the Scottish version and then trying the 'Chance in France' poem in pairs or small groups.

Writing
- Use an atlas or local map to list place-names that might be useful. It is important to collect names that have potential rhymes.
- Work as a class to use the same sort of pattern and invent some together before children continue on their own, e.g. 'I was loud/in Stroud . . .'

Notes for page 10: language play ('The Zealous Zoo')

Reading
- What do the children notice – who knows what the technique is called?
- Read and discuss each line.
- Vote for favourites – explain why you like that one!

Writing
- Make a list of animals.
- Work as a class to build alliterative sentences by putting words before and after the name of the creature to complete a sentence.
- When the children write on their own, add in the competitive element of seeing who can write the sentence with the most alliteration!

Notes for page 11: language play ('Collective Poem')

Reading
- Read the poem through – ask the children to explain the poem.
- Explain and discuss collective nouns.
- Those in the first half of the poem are traditional – so too are the jays, kittens, finches, sharks, toads and yaks. In the second half some have been invented to rhyme.

Writing
- Make a list of possible subjects and invent collective nouns together, e.g. a weariness of teachers, a chuckle of children, a sheep of clouds, a float of tents, etc. It doesn't matter if they don't quite make sense – the more mysterious the better. The more able may use rhyme but this is not necessary.
- Let the children invent their own.

Notes for page 12: language play ('The Obstinate Ostrich')

Reading
- Read and discuss each verse – annotate, underlining key words such as powerful verbs.

74

Teachers' notes

- Ask the class to work in pairs to discuss 'what is missing' – you could provide a clue. (Each verse has one of the vowels missing, in order a, e, i, o, u). This is a 'Univolic'.

Writing
- Work together to write a sentence about a creature, omitting one vowel.
- Let the children continue.
- Not as easy as it sounds!

Notes for page 14: language play ('Nonsense Poem')

Reading
- Let the children work in pairs to prepare a reading.
- Does anyone know the traditional rhyme that this is based upon (I went to the animal fair . . .)?
- What might each nonsense word mean?

Writing
- Use the same pattern or another well-known verse.
- Write the verse out as it originally stood.
- Swap some nouns and verbs for invented words.
- In pairs, prepare and perform.

Notes for page 15: language play ('Animal Riddle')

Reading
- Who can work out the answer? Each line provides clues to a letter?
- The final line provides an overall clue.
- Answer = t-i-g-e-r.

Writing
- Demonstrate how to write a riddle using the same pattern. Choose an animal, e.g. cat.
- Create an opening line based on the letter 'c', e.g. 'My first is in pick but never in nose'.
- When writing the second line, more able children will want to use a rhyme – but this is not necessary, e.g. 'My second is in grab but never in hold'.
- It may be worth listing a few animals before starting – cat, dog, rat, flea, etc.

STORY MODELS

Notes for page 16: stories in familiar settings (dialogue)

Reading
- Read each example and discuss how the writer has set out the dialogue – make a wall chart of basic rules.
- Discuss how the writer shows the character – by what is said, use of speech verb, use of adverb.
- There are five extracts – work out strategies for writing dialogue to avoid a stream of speech, e.g.
  1. Think about how the character is feeling and therefore what they might say.
  2. Use a powerful speech verb.
  3. Use 'said' plus an adverb.
  4. Add in a supporting action to show what the characters are doing as they speak. Use a comma and 'ing' clause to do this.
  5. Add in what the listener is doing and background details. These can be separate sentences.
  6. Show or suggest how characters feel, e.g.' Mr Ramsbotham . . . and winced.'

Teachers' notes

Writing

- As a class, practise using strategies for avoiding speech streams by adding in a supporting action and so forth. Work on this bit by bit so that there is not too much to remember.
- Some groups may only get as far as using a powerful speech verb or 'said' plus an adverb.

Notes for page 18: settings ('The Giant Man' and 'Strawberry Banks')

1. The Giant Man: in the style of The Iron Man
Reading

- This is based upon the rhythm of the first two chapters of Ted Hughes' great book. The whole book does not take long to read and every child should have heard of it.
- Look carefully at the pattern of sentences – can the children sketch the picture being described?

Writing

- Imitate the pattern by copying the sentence openings and rhythm – 'She/he looked . . .', 'Beyond the . . . was the . . .', etc.
- End the description by having a monster or creature. It can help to sketch the scene first of all.
- Encourage the children to use a known local place.

2. Strawberry Banks
Reading

- Identify the way the writer has used the senses.
- Choose a well-known place and list what you can see, hear, smell, feel.
- Take each thing you can see and show how to add to this, e.g. field – green field – green field of grass – green field of grass blowing in the breeze.
- Of course, when describing settings it helps to take the class to the place and make notes on-site.

Notes for pages 20 and 22: examples of openings and endings

Reading

- Match the openings to their partner endings. How did you know?
- Categorise and label the openings – place, name of character, time, dialogue, traditional, action.
- Discuss how the openings suggest a story.
- Discuss tactics for endings, e.g. traditional, take the main character home, what has been learned, hinting at the next story, using the weather to suggest the end, finding a friend.

Writing

- As a class, imitate the different types of opening, e.g. 'On the other side of the road stood a strange house/Eddie Ingot was miserable/Once there was a sailor who lost his ship./Sal sneaked into the chip shop when no one was looking./"Let's take it," said Si, looking at the donut hungrily./Late one dark night, when the moon was hidden behind clouds, Chang left home.'
- Children then invent their own.

Notes for page 24: story with familiar setting ('One Sweet Too Far')

Reading

- Get the children to tease out the basic plot – ask them to write in six boxes what is happening in the story – opening, hides and eats, Billy arrives, asks for sweet, Alfie fools him, Billy gets caught.
- Draw attention to the use of powerful verbs (e.g. 'popped', 'leaning', 'eyed', 'shoved'.
- Look at the use of the dialogue to suggest the sort of person that Billy might be.

Teachers' notes

Writing
- Use the same structure – opening in which character has something, goes off to use it, someone horrid tries to take it, main character tricks them, ending.
- Discuss local place where story might be set.

Notes for pages 26–29: story with familiar setting ('You Can Have Your Cake . . .')

Reading
- In what ways is this story similar to the previous one?
- How does the writer emphasise that the cake must be saved?
- Box up the plot (opening, gets cake, heads for home, gets attacked, made to walk plank, Slugger falls in, runs off, end) – then explain how Mitch's feelings change, and why.
- How does the ending relate to the beginning?
- Search for powerful and well-chosen verbs; discuss impact.
- Look at dialogue to see how it reflects character.

Writing
- Agree on a local place where a key event from a story might occur and brainstorm words/phrases for description.
- Use the same frame to plot a story – opening, main character has something precious, others try to get it away, main character manages to keep precious item, end.
- Story needs reasons why object cannot be given away – also, try to tie up end with start.

Notes for pages 30–32: plays

Reading
- In groups of four, children should work to prepare a reading or to act out the scene provided.
- Discuss the characters and what is known about them.
- Identify the conventions of a play.

Writing
- What might happen next? (Does the package disappear and Bobby get the blame?)
- In groups of four, discuss ideas and improvise the next scene.
- In groups, children plot out and write three more scenes, based on improvisations.

Notes for page 34: traditional tale ('The Magic Brush')

Reading
- Plot the structure onto a simple storyboard.
  - Opening – main character is kind to creature.
  - Creature returns in dream and grants a wish.
  - Main character does good deeds.
  - Greedy tyrant makes main character use magic.
  - Main character tricks tyrant.
  - End.
- Identify and collect typical words and phrases that might be re-used, e.g. 'Long, long ago . . .'

Writing
- Discuss other ideas for setting, e.g. forest, mountain cave, etc.
- What does main character desire/need, e.g. magic pencil, crayon, pen, quill.
- What creature might be helped?
- Describe dream sequence.
- What good deeds are carried out?

Teachers' notes

- What does tyrant ask main character to do?
- How does main character trick tyrant?
- How will it end?
- Draw ideas on storyboard or picture map.
- Children tell own tales in pairs before writing.

Notes for pages 36–37: traditional tale ('The King of the Fishes')

Reading
- Discuss ways in which this story is similar to 'The Magic Brush'.
- In small groups act out the story, using mime and words.
- Storyboard the sequence like a cartoon.
- Identify and collect words and phrases that might be re-used.

Writing.
- Extract basic plot and write own version by:
  - altering setting, e.g. harbour, river bank, lakeside, field, mountainside, etc.
  - instead of a fish it could be a unicorn (eagle, etc.) that gets saved and grants a wish.
  - asking three different people, e.g. brother, sister, old aunt.
- Use same trick at the end.

Notes for page 38: fable ('The Fox and the Raven')

Reading
- What does the story mean?
- Discuss the two characters.
- Explain the trick.
- Discuss and list the features of a fable – brief tale, about creatures, moral at end.

Writing
- Re-write the tale but alter the setting and characters.
- Keep the same basic trick by using flattery.
- Notice and re-use the idea of repetitive language.

Notes for page 40: fable ('The Mouse and the Lion')

Reading
- Draw the basic plot onto a story mountain, e.g. tiny creature is out, gets caught by big creature, tiny creature pleads and big creature feels sorry, big creature releases tiny creature, big creature gets captured, tiny creature repays the debt and releases big creature.
- Identify the three key connectives that can structure the turning points of the tale, e.g. 'One night . . .', 'Later that night . . .', 'While . . .'

Writing
- List ideas for a different pair of creatures that vary in size – these could be animals, birds, fish, etc.
- Children should take their new ideas and retell their version before writing.

Teachers' notes

Notes for page 41: myth ('Why Spider Has a Small Waist')

Reading
- This myth explains 'Why' rather than 'How'.
- Discuss the character of Spider as shown by the tale.

Writing
- List other creatures that have distinctive features, e.g. giraffe's long neck, elephant's trunk, etc.
- Discuss ideas that might explain how this happened.
- Draw a storyboard and tell own tale before writing.

Notes for page 42: myth ('How the World Was Made')

Reading
- Discuss main features of a myth (the 'How' or 'Why' of the world) and identify the pattern in this one.
- Identify useful words and phrases.

Writing
- Make a list with two columns. In the first column list the different aspects of the world that need to be 'brought alive', e.g. the clouds, the sun, the night, the trees, etc. Opposite list the instrument that might perform this function.
- Tell and retell own versions before writing, using same pattern.
- Some might alter pattern, e.g. 'On Monday the piper . . .'

Notes for page 44: character portrait

Reading
- Which story is this based on?
- What does Monkey think of Spider's behaviour – how do you know?

Writing
- Write own version but change the tone of the letter by having the correspondent feel sorry for Spider.
- Before writing, sit children in pairs, back to back. They make a phone call about the event in role as creatures!

Notes for page 46: character portrait

Reading
- Notice the function of different paragraphs – physical description, what he does, where he lives, what happened.

Writing
- Use the same pattern but base the letter on children's own versions.
- Other ways – character passport, drawing plus description, 'Wanted' notice.

Notes for page 47: sequel to traditional tale ('The King of the Fishes')

Reading
- Extract the plot – main character helps creature – main character gets in trouble – creature repays debt.
- Extract plot onto seven-part sequence – identify key connectives that start the paragraphs.
- Which story does this echo?

Teachers' notes

Writing
- Reuse same basic plot but with different ideas.
- Use connectives to write a seven-paragraph/section story – once, every day, one day, that afternoon, suddenly, at that moment, eventually.

Notes for page 48: sequel to traditional tale ('The Magic Brush')

Reading
- Use a story mountain or storyboard or list to map out the main events.
- Draw attention to simple five-part pattern (one paragraph per part) – opening, build up, problem (suddenly), resolution, ending.
- List the relevant connectives – 'Once . . .', 'One day . . .', 'Suddenly . . .', 'So . . .', 'Finally . . .'.

Writing
- Write own sequel in which Chang has to use the brush/pen to save the village from someone or thing that is horrible.
- Plan on story mountain or storyboard a five-part plot.
- Reuse same five-part sequence and connectives to aid writing in paragraphs.

Notes for pages 50–52: adventures and mysteries (openings)

Reading
- Discuss and categorise different openings.
- Ask children to say which they think are most effective (make you want to read on/create an atmosphere, etc.) and explain why.

Writing
- Imitate different types of opening as a class and individually.
- This could be done on whiteboards.
- Make a class list of different types and make sure these are used in children's own stories.

Notes for pages 54–55: first-person account of incident in story read

Reading
- Can children guess the stories that these are based on?
- Reread original versions – Chapter 9 in *James and the Giant Peach* (p. 54) and the start of Chapter 2 in *The Iron Man* (p. 55).
- Notice differences, e.g. use of first person.

Writing
- Take a key moment from a story being read to the class.
- Hot-seat a child in role.
- Ask children to monologue events – or tell class what has just happened, in role as the character, using 'I'.
- It can help to box the scene/events so that paragraphs will be used. Try adding on connectives or paragraphs starters to assist weaker writers.
- Children write first-person accounts.

Teachers' notes

Notes for pages 56–58: opening chapter of an extended mystery story ('The Mystery of the Lantern Light' and 'The Mystery of the Ottoman's Chest')

Reading
- Discuss basic six chapter plots for a mystery.
- Read examples of opening chapters.
- Notice how writer builds up to the mysterious element by describing something normal like walking the dog or eating a packed lunch.
- Discuss the characters and what is known about them – what sort of people are they?

Writing
- Either of these could be continued.
- Children could work in groups of six, taking a chapter each – or work on their own extended story.
- Begin by fleshing out a plot on the board – who are the main characters, where are they, what are they doing that is normal, what do they see that is out of place/mysterious?

Notes for pages 59–60: book review (*The BFG* and *The Iron Man*)

Reading
- Read both examples.
- Which is better, and why?
- Discuss own views of the stories.
- Tease out structure – introduce book, what is it about, likes/dislikes, conclusion.
- Notice paragraph openers – 'The . . . is . . .', 'The story is about . . .', 'I liked . . .', 'In conclusion . . .'

Writing
- Take well-known class book.
- Use same framework to write class version.
- Children prepare an oral review using the same framework. They should also read a short and exciting extract to the class!
- Make sure that they choose a book that they think the class will enjoy. No one wants to review a dull book.
- Children write own review of book they have enjoyed.

NON-FICTION MODELS

Notes for pages 62–64: non-chronological report ('Unicorns' and 'Dragons')

Reading
- Before reading, list – what you know.
- Read and add new information to list.
- How are the passages organised – give subheadings to each paragraph, e.g. 'What it is' (definition), 'What it looks like' (description), 'Where it is found' (location), 'What it eats' (lifestyle), 'What it is best known for', 'Most amazing fact'.
- Note the language features, e.g. present tense ('Hamsters are . . .', 'It is . . .') and factual tone.
- Make a wall chart that includes the paragraph headings and language features.

Writing
- With the class, select a creature they know about.
- Under the paragraph headings list information.
- Add to it from reference material available.

Teachers' notes

- Children use this to write their own report in paragraphs.
- They could then move on to selecting a creature that they are interested in – gather information, organise under the headings and write.

Notes for pages 65–66: instructions ('How to Make a Traditional Story' and 'How to Trap a Troll')

Reading
- Read and discuss.
- How are the texts organised – give subheadings to each section, e.g. 'How to . . .' title, introduction, what you need, what to do, end paragraph.
- Note the language features, e.g. use of colon and commas, alphabet, connectives to order what is done, 'bossy' verbs ('place', 'boil', 'start', etc.).
- Make a wall chart that includes subheadings and language features.

Writing
- With the class, select a topic that they know about, e.g. how to turn the computer on.
- Under the subheadings note or draw.
- Children use this to write their own instructions.
- They could then move on to selecting an imaginative idea of their own, e.g. how to trap a giant.

Notes for pages 68–70: same event – recount letter, and same event – diary ('Letter About Hare and Tortoise's Race', 'Tortoise's Diary' and 'Hare's Diary')

Reading
- Read the diaries of the hare and tortoise on page 70.
- Read the three pieces and discuss.
- Pick up clues about the different characters from what they say or do.
- Underline the temporal connectives in the letter and check if there are any useful ones in the diary entries.
- Make a note of the basic structure and list this on a wall chart, e.g.:
  - Introduction – when, who, where, why.
  - What happened in order.
  - End paragraph comments on events.
- Make a note of language features, e.g. temporal connectives, past tense, detail and comments about what happened, etc.

Writing
- Choose a story that is known well. You could use a traditional tale such as Red Riding Hood or 'The King of the Fishes' on page 36.
- Draw a storyboard, timeline or sequence using a flow-chart for the events. Make a note at the start of when, who, where and why. Add in final comment.
- Discuss writing about the events in role, e.g. as a woodcutter.
- Children use this as a plan for their own writing, choosing a letter or diary format. Remind them to consider the difference between letter and diary in terms of audience and style.
- Other recounts could be written about memories, school, events or based on events in the class story.

Teachers' notes

Notes for pages 71–72: alphabetically ordered text (from 'The Encyclopaedia of Nasty Creatures' and from the long-lost 'Rough Guide to Fantasyland')

Reading
- Read and discuss contents.
- Note similarities – alphabetical order, rather like a mini report on each topic.
- Note different tone to rough guide which addresses the traveller more directly.

Writing
- Decide on a curriculum area that might make a useful focus for an encyclopaedic text, e.g. The Romans.
- As a class, list an alphabet of headings, e.g.
  - Armour,
  - Barbarians,
  - Centurion.
- Individuals can take different sections.
- They should gather information about their given topic, and write a brief entry plus illustration. If each child creates a page these could be made into a class book on the topic.

Looking for creative and imaginative ways to teach writing, speaking and listening?

Here's the solution you've been waiting for...

NEW!

SPEAKING FRAMES

by Sue Palmer

Here's an effective and innovative answer to the problem of how to teach speaking and listening. By orally 'filling in' a speaking frame children will learn to listen to, imitate, make innovations with, and invent language patterns.

These books will:

- save teachers time with photocopiable sheets
- help teaching in groups, pairs and one-to-one
- support teachers with accompanying notes
- guide teachers on assessment

NEW!

WRITING MODELS

by Pie Corbett

Are you looking for creative and imaginative models to help you teach writing? This series provides all you need!

Each book in the series gives you:

- a bank of easy to use, photocopiable models for writing covering poetry, fiction and non-fiction for each year group at Key Stage 2
- key teaching points for each model
- simpler and harder examples for differentiation

← *Sample page from Writing models*

Speaking Frames - Year 3

- Show and tell frames for individual use (a tool or utensil; a personal treasure)
- 'We're thinking of...' frames for paired work (an object, an animal, a place)
- 'How to...' frames for groupwork (making something, following rules, using your imagination)

£12.00 • 80 pages • 1-84312-109-3 • March 2004

Speaking Frames - Year 4

- 'My favourite...' frames for individual use (book, TV programme, poem)
- 'Check it out' frames for paired work (planning research, a non-fiction book, paragraphs and key words)
- 'Four points' frames for group work ('Four good uses for a...', 'Four ways we would change...', 'Four people we'd invite to school')

£12.00 • 80 A4 pages • 1-84312-110-7 • March 2004

Writing Models - Year 3

- Stories in familiar setting, traditional tales, adventures and mysteries
- Poems about the senses, observation, performance and word play
- Reports, instructions, various letters and plays

£12.00 • 96 pages • 1-84312-094-1 • February 2004

Writing Models - Year 4

- Poems based on common themes and in different forms
- Historical stories, sci-fi and fantasy, stories with issues, and plays
- Newspaper reporting, instructions, explanations, discussions and persuasive writing

£12.00 • 96 A4 pages • 1-84312-095-X • March 2004

David Fulton Publishers ▪ The Chiswick Centre ▪ 414 Chiswick High Road ▪ London W4 5TF
Tel : 0208 996 3610 ▪ Fax: 0208 996 3622 ▪ orders@fultonpublishers.co.uk ▪ www.fultonpublishers.co.uk

Speaking Frames - Year 5

- 'In my opinion' frames for individual use ('There should be a law...', 'The greatest person who ever lived...', '...should be banned!')

- 'Tell the aliens' frames for paired work ('How it works', 'What it is', 'How to play (a team game)')

- Compare and contrast frames for group work

£12.00 • 80 A4 pages • 1-84312-111-5 • March 2004

Writing Models - Year 5

- Poetry using metaphor, creating moods, narrative and performance;

- Traditional tales, cliff hangers, thrillers and playscripts

- Recounts, instructions, reports and explanations

£12.00 • 96 A4 pages • 1-84312-096-8 • March 2004

Speaking Frames - Year 6

- Recount frames for individual use ('My life so far', 'A great life', 'A science experiment')

- Critical evaluation frames for paired work (fiction book, poem, non-fiction text)

- Points of view frames for group work ('A major controversy', 'Order of importance', 'What if?')

£12.00 • 80 A4 pages • 1-84312-112-3 • March 2004

Writing Models - Year 6

- Poems in different forms, sequences and handling personification

- Modern retellings, mysteries, adventures, fantasy, sci-fi, and flashbacks

- Biography and autobiography, journalism, reports, discussions and formal writing

£12.00 • 96 A4 pages • 1-84312-097-6 • April 2004

Money Back Guarantee!
All our books are supplied on a 28 day invoice. If they're unsuitable just return them and we'll cancel the invoice.

ORDER FORM

Qty	ISBN	Title	Price	Subtotal
	1-84312-109-3	Speaking Frames Year 3	£12.00	
	1-84312-110-7	Speaking Frames Year 4	£12.00	
	1-84312-111-5	Speaking Frames Year 5	£12.00	
	1-84312-112-3	Speaking Frames Year 6	£12.00	
	1-84312-094-1	Writing Models Year 3	£12.00	
	1-84312-095-X	Writing Models Year 4	£12.00	
	1-84312-096-8	Writing Models Year 5	£12.00	
	1-84312-097-6	Writing Models Year 6	£12.00	
			P&P	
			TOTAL	

Postage and Packing: FREE to Schools, LEAs and other institutions. £2.50 for orders to private addresses. Prices and publication dates are subject to change.

Payment

☐ Please invoice (applicable to schools, LEAs and other institutions) *Invoices will be sent from our distributor.*

☐ I enclose a cheque payable to David Fulton Publishers Ltd *(include postage and packing)*

☐ Please charge to my credit card (Visa/Barclaycard, Access/Mastercard, American Express, Switch, Delta)

card number ☐☐☐☐ ☐☐☐☐ ☐☐☐☐ ☐☐☐☐ ☐☐☐☐

expiry date ☐☐☐☐

(Switch customers only) valid from ☐☐☐☐ issue number ☐

Please complete delivery details

Name: ....

Organisation: ....

....

Address: ....

....

....

....

Postcode: ....

Tel: ....

To order

Send to:
David Fulton Publishers,
The Chiswick Centre
414 Chiswick High Road
London W4 5TF

Freecall:
020 8996 3610

Fax:
020 8996 3622

www.fultonpublishers.co.uk